POWER OF 21:
Pathways Towards a Brighter Future

First published in the United Kingdom by:
Darren Douglas Publishers

Copyright © 2018 Darren Douglas

Darren Douglas has asserted his right under the Copyright, Designs
and Patents Act 1988 to be identified as the author of this work.

Logo Design: Teodora Popa
Project Management & Production: OWN IT! Entertainment Ltd

ISBN: 9781527227736

Darren Douglas
Email: powerof21@outlook.com
Twitter: @DarrenDouglas_
Instagram: @powerof21online

In loving memory of
Lewis Elwin

Contents

AUTHOR'S INTRODUCTION

My name is Darren Douglas and I am a qualified former Youth Worker. I've had the pleaure of working with young people from diverse backgrounds for various projects and organisations including YMCA East London, Roundhouse, Arsenal Community Kickz, National Youth Theatre, People's Palace Project and more.

I decided to put together a book for young people titled the 'Power of 21 - Pathways Towards A Brighter Future' as I wanted to leave behind a message, legacy and contribution in the form of an inspirational toolkit before I ended my service as a Youth Worker to the community and society as a whole and move onto the next chapter of my life.

My hope is that this book will help guide, motivate and influence, not only the young people I've come into contact with over the last 7 years but the hundreds of thousands of young citizens nationwide.

Throughout 2015 I was doing a lot of soul searching

as I was looking for a new challenge and purpose in life. I wanted to create and explore new and exciting opportunities but also start a project from the ground up and see it through to completion, combining my skills, experience and the passion I have for working with young people and helping them increase their confidence to achieve their aspirations.

During countless conversations with young people across various projects/sessions I've facilitated, I would hear lots of encouraging signs of the progress they were making in their hobbies, extra-curricular activities (outside of study time) and careers. But coupled with this I would also hear great annoyance and frustration in regards to the limited information, advice and guidance available to them from individuals already working, established and recognised across various industries/professions they were interested in pursuing or finding out more about.

As much as Google is a great friend to have, it does not always have the answers young people are looking for. I want to help bridge that gap, find that missing piece of the puzzle to the queries which are not always answered and get young people in tune to the psyche of the current trailblazers leading the way in their field. Not only in terms of what they did and how they separated themselves from the crowd but also in terms of understanding the hard work, dedication and sacrifice it took to be where they are today.

On Monday 18th April 2016, my step brother Lewis

Elwin died at the hands of knife crime. This tragic ordeal reinforced my passion for this project and the importance of helping to empower young people throughout the country to pursue positive pathways towards a brighter future.

Writing the Power of 21 has played a massive part in my own personal development and has given me the opportunity to meet and interview some truly inspirational role models.

In this book I share their advice and insights in the hope that it will help to affect positive change in young people's lives.

ZAWE ASHTON

Actress, Writer and Director

'An important pitfall for young people to avoid is 'Don't believe the hype!''

Zawe Ashton – Prelude

Zawe Ashton is an actress, playwright and director best known for her roles in the Channel 4 comedy dramas Not Safe for Work and Fresh Meat. Other credits include the feature films Blitz and St Trinian's 2: The Legend of Fritton's Gold.

ZAWE ASHTON INTERVIEW

Where it Began:

I started acting professionally at the age of six years old. I went to a local drama class called the Anna Scher Theatre in Islington, which had an agency attached to it. It was one of the best places to go at that time as it was not only affordable but it was on Friday night and Saturday afternoons so it didn't interfere with your normal schooling. It was a hub for any child of all walks of life and not exclusive in any way. I did my first class at 5 years old and instantly loved it, I just knew that this was the world for me. Just having those classes as a hobby blossomed into professional work and I've been very lucky that this has constantly continued throughout my career.

At age nineteen I decided that I wanted to train professionally as I began to feel there were some obstacles I was facing in terms of type casting. The roles that I was playing were starting to become repetitive and didn't feel interesting or nourishing and I didn't want to fall into a pattern of work that indulges negative stereotypes, generally with regard to people of colour and more importantly women of colour. After coming out of drama school and back into the professional world I had to start from scratch again and I was very lucky to be suggested by someone from the National Youth Theatre to be put forward to audition for a play at the Royal Court Theatre called 'Gone Too Far' which is still one of the most special projects I've been a part of and really enabled acting to be one of my main sources of income today.

Mum, Dad and Will Smith

Both my mum and dad supported my decision very early on in life to become an Actor. So my acting journey starts with them because I've seen people be discouraged and dissuaded to do the job they really want because it's too precarious. To have two parents from day one who 100% supported my need to be part of an artistic world and make that into my career and future was very lucky.

Professionally, Will Smith was a hugely iconic role model for me. I had a real affiliation with him and he was very inspiring for me to watch on TV. Fresh Prince of Bel Air was one of the only shows we had playing on UK television where the characters looked like my family, people I knew or from my own community (even though they were living in a mansion in Beverley Hill.) He represented black life through the prism of art that was written, directed and structured for our enjoyment to connect with. He was the driving force behind this show and an absolute all-rounder. He seemed to be doing everything, music, acting and comedy, whilst being so young as well.

Comic Relief

My biggest success is just staying in work, achieving this hasn't been easy. It's just been about tenacity, patience, a lot of self-care and love and having a very positive community of family and friends around me.

A real personal success was when I was asked by Comic Relief to do a documentary for them on Female Genital Mutilation in the UK and in Kenya. That was one of the first times when my profile and publicity as an Actor was recognised on the level of activism I do. When these two worlds came together it was a real life changing experience for me. I went and spent 2 weeks out living with the Masai in Kenya, which is not something anyone really gets the opportunity to do and so to be able to make a piece of work that's helpful to that community, thousands of miles away, in my heartland of Africa (my Mother is Ugandan, and Kenya is next door) and connect with British women who'd experienced this practice and were surviving, was very transcending for me as a person.

Write Your Own Material

There was a time specifically at Drama School when I was trying to find a monologue piece for my end of year showcase in front of industry representatives. I found it so hard to find a piece that encapsulated me as a young woman of colour from London. I literally felt that when I was going through the library of all these monologue books/plays; the whole theatrical world was against me. None of those plays were speaking specifically to me or included half a page where I could choose a character that seemed to be coming from the mouth of someone like myself. The support from Drama School was quite minimal when it came to this and so it felt like I was facing a wall of adversity and that there wasn't any way I could properly showcase myself at this event because of the lack of material. Fortunately, I did find a wonderful monologue in the end but it was from a play written and performed many years ago, and so encountering this problem prompted and motivated me to get on my laptop and start writing my own material.

In the first ever play I wrote Harms Way, all 3 characters in the play were people of colour. The play went on to be nominated for the Verity Bargate Award at the Soho Theatre. On reflection, I found that I turned that moment of adversity into a positive and was moving the problem forward in my own way. Adversity seems to be a continual driving force in my life and career. I feel not only committed in the art that I do but also to the social change that I would like to see in my community too. There's nothing like getting a bit angry to get the focus sharpened.

Preparation

A daily routine if I'm making a TV show would be different to that of theatre, film or writing etc. Routine's that I would regularly incorporate into my preparation for all of those are; doing as much reading and research as possible around the area/topic I'm working on and putting together all the technical bits I would need prepared to be ready for a role/job. Music is another big part of my preparation. I will always have a playlist for a piece of writing that I'm doing or character that I'm creating. Exercise is important too, particularly yoga. I've found I'm much more engaged when I have some level of spiritual practice to what I do. The Philosopher Carl Jung once said "learn your techniques well and be prepared to let them go when you touch the human soul". How I interpret that is to prepare as much as possible but also prepare to let it all go when you touch the human soul and connect to something truthful.

Getting Perspective

I've been acting for such a long time now that I've realised I've sacrificed so much in the pursuit of everything that I do. You do have to absolutely be bloody minded and pig headed when it comes to this industry because there is so much competition. You have to work extremely hard and be focused to get to where you want to get to, and that does come at a really great sacrifice to your social and family life. It is something I definitely do struggle to find a balance on but what I do now is give myself perspective and say to myself "It's all about the work, do your work, have focused time with your work and then you'll always have focus time with your family and friends."

Don't Believe The Hype!
I think an important pitfall for young people to avoid is 'Don't believe the hype!' Get to know yourself and work on yourself, whatever that might mean for you. You don't have to run with the crowd, there's not a big idea of some person that you're supposed to be. Just get inside your instincts and really nurture that because any work that you do will grow from that.

Read as much as you can as it's the only way to know anything about this world. Get to know what you like. As an Actor, I have a very strong sense of my own ethics and I'm very glad about that as it helps me navigate my work. In my life, I try to be as honest as I can with people even if it's painful because I need to experience real truth and pain if I want to be able to access it in my work.

Give Your Own Individual Performance
When you go into the room as an actress no one is looking for you to do the same performance as 10 other people, they're only looking for the performance that you are going to do as an individual. Ten thousand people could audition for Hamlet, each one of them could do it

differently so it's about connecting to your own truth and finding your own way into the material and not thinking "how am I supposed to do it?" or to please the crowd because there is no right way.

The truth is universal, if you look at someone like Martin Luther King and see the way he was able to lead, speak and connect with people, and start a movement where people were willing to put themselves in mortal danger for a common cause, it moves you and inspires you. That is the level of meaning and connection I'm looking to get to with any script that I'm working on.

Invest!
When it comes to the acting industry I would advise to save as much money as you can and make as many investments as you can whether that be in property, nice pieces of clothing, a great showreel or headshots. Always invest in something that will last because no bank statements from one year to another will be the same especially when you're starting out as a professional.

Finding My Groove In College
My level of education has contributed a great deal on lots of different levels. I think I really came into myself at college. School can leave you a bit institutionalised, college really dropped me down into myself, I found my groove and that was invaluable as I really developed as an adult and that definitely paid dividends in my work. I had fantastic teachers and social groups and met people that really inspired me and changed my outlook on life and got me to know myself so much better. Going to drama School and living outside of London as a Londoner was

quite significant and a healthy thing for me to do because I learnt the skills I needed in order to have longevity in my career.

TOP TIPS

1. Get involved; there is no Youth/Theatre Group too small or time consuming. Get as much experience as you can.

2. Be proactive; if you've got a group of friends, get together and write your own material. Always have your own sense of agency within the industry. It's not an industry that will necessarily work for you if you're sitting waiting for the phone to ring for an audition or a job.

3. To be an actor/actress you have to develop such a thick skin. Decide why you're in it and doing it because it's a really hard profession. The only thing that's going to get you through it is how much dedication you are willing to give to it.

4. Lastly, don't just make your life about acting, make it about lots of other things that you're passionate about and that turns you on.

I WOULD LIKE TO BE REMEMBERED AS...

An Artistic Social Worker who helped bring about positive changes within the acting industry and society as a whole through the work that I do in my art form.

ZAWE ASHTON PATHWAY PITSTOPS

• Turn your moments of adversity into positives

• Read and research as much as possible when working on a project or preparing for a role.
• Don't believe the hype!
• Create a strong sense of your own ethics
• Connect your own truth to a script and find your own way into the material for performance
• Save and invest as much money as you can
• Be proactive and get as much experience as possible when starting out

ZAWE ASHTON CONTACT DETAILS

Twitter: @ZaweAshton
Instagram: @Zawe

KELVIN OKAFOR

Artist

'I found that rather than wanting life to give me something, I asked what more could I give to life?'

Kelvin Okafor Prelude

Kelvin Okafor is an award winning Portrait Artist from Tottenham, North London. His work can be seen exhibited in Houses of Parliament and in many prestigious galleries throughout the U.K. He has won many awards including the Catherine Petitgas Visitors Choice Prize, part of the National Open Art Competition.

KELVIN OKAFOR INTERVIEW

My name is Kelvin Okafor and I am a Professional Artist. I was born and bred in Tottenham north London and I believe I am a spiritual being out of consciousness.

Fascination for Drawing and the Hardships of Homelessness

I was 8 years old when I vividly remember having that love and fascination for drawing with pencils. There was something about the humble instrument of a pencil. It's one shade of lead but then it creates different tones and textures. I saw an illusion of colour even though it was black or just a grey tone and that inspired me. For the rest of my early years I spent a lot of time utilising its full use and before I knew it I was completely in love with this material. Seeing the impact it gave others, gave me the courage to continue using it.

When I was eleven years old my life took a turn for the hard end. My mum's father passed away and so we went to Nigeria to bury him and when we got back our house was repossessed and we were unfortunately homeless for the following 7 years. Throughout that period of time we were living in different relative's houses with so much uncertainty, and unfortunately it led to me having severe depression to points where I had thoughts of suicide. However, whilst going through this it brought me even closer to drawing. What art then became for me was an outlet, a way for me to purge and rid myself of negative emotions and to go into another universe where it was just me, and all that I could ever want and wish for was there in that moment whilst I was creating.

My Influences

My mum is a huge inspiration to me. She's a warrior and a truly strong human being. Despite us going through such uncertainty, never having that comfort and peace of mind of knowing where we would be living, she made us hope and that hope I truly believe pulled us through our darkest times.

Growing up my idols and inspiration was Boys 2 Men. It was more than just the love songs. The technicality of their voices and the passion that they had for their craft and music inspired me to pursue the love that I had for it too. Football was another incredible passion of mine and I was inspired by Ian Wright. I played for Arsenal Juniors until I tore both ligaments in my knees which crushed my dreams at fifteen. But whatever it was I had an interest in, I always tried to maximise it. Football was a dream and something I wanted to do until my knees gave way, and then music was there and then when that gave way art was there.

My Statement

Fortunately, there were many occasions of adversity and hardship. The reason I say fortunately is because I believe going through adversity and hardship strengthens and deepens you as a human being and there are lots of lessons that you learn in that process. When things are all going good for you, yes life is wonderful and everything is manifesting the way you want but there are not many lessons for you to learn.

After graduating from university with a Fine Art degree in 2009, I knew that at the end of it that this is what I wanted to do but I had no idea as to how I could make a living, I just wanted to build my portfolio.

On September 12th 2012, I wrote down a financial statement and a statement of what I was going to give in return. "I intend to acquire £100,000 by May 5th 2013. I intend to give my talents freely inspiring and encouraging others in return for the money. Help my family and loved ones with fiscal, financial and emotional difficulties. My plan is to build my portfolio, to have my art work touring, sold in prestigious galleries and exhibitions, winning awards and having my works commissioned" I would say this first thing in the morning and last thing at night before I retire and would keep a rota of the money I accumulated to keep track of my goal.

In the following weeks ahead, I browsed the internet and looked for open exhibitions where I could submit and exhibit my art work and soon was featured in the Mall Gallery, then the Vibe Gallery – where I won the Visitors Choice Award which the publically voted for. My work was selected to win out of two hundred and fifty artists. I was thankful and really emotional as there was money that came with the prize.

By the end of December that year I had attracted the Vanguard Newspaper in Nigeria who wanted to do a press article on me and in turn led to a Nigerian High Commissioner Dr Emmanuel Eweta Uduaghan commissioning my work.

Early into the New Year things started to pick up dramatically, my social media audience was growing and out of the blue I received an email from Shazia Mowlabaccus, a press officer from my former university about the prospect of becoming an Alumni member. Days later I then won another award at the Gallery in Cork Street and was asked by the university if they could film me at the exhibition receiving the award. Shazia, sent press outlets everywhere, to the BBC, regional and national newspapers so that they were aware of me. Then, in that same week I went back to my former university to do a masterclass which the BBC wanted to film me doing. During the masterclass, I featured on the BBC London News segment and from there boom! Everything changed in my life. My phone could not stop ringing. By May 4th 2013 I had acquired £87,000 and the next day on May 5th I had acquired, in total £107,000 and had surpassed my target and for me that was so unbelievable.

From all the adversity I faced in my early teens to then seeking how I could help myself, I found that rather than wanting life to give me something, I asked what more could I give to life and that was how my statement came about.

Breaking News!

My biggest success is having the courage to continue to draw after leaving university. Each of my drawings take a hundred hours to complete and so having a drawing completed is great success for me especially within those 2-3 weeks when nothing was coming in financially and I was just working off of raw love and passion despite my struggles. In terms of the conceptual term of success I would say it was in 2013 appearing on BBC London News. That moment for me enabled me to pursue this career as an Artist because of what it brought to me financially and the fulfilment of the goal being to inspire others and enabling me to have that reach.

Work Ethic & Routines

During and after university I had to develop discipline. Having been in schooling my whole life I now knew I had to develop some sort of structure to my day. So, I wake up at 5.30am every morning and meditate and pray for 30mins, so spiritually I'm deepened and ready to embark on the day. I'll take a short break then read for 2 hours and then break again. I then prepare myself to stretch and work out for 2 hours. At around 10/11am I start to draw for 4 hours and then take a 1 hour break and repeat that sequence throughout the rest of the day. I usually draw for twelve hours in total. Working out and reading definitely helps and prepares me for the task. Reading relaxes and strengths my eye muscles and working out strengthens the physical body. I specialise in very high detailed work so it forces me to be very attentive to detail. Every moment of the day is very precious and I try to be as present as I can in the moment.

Sacrifices Are Required

Something that I enjoy doing, I give my undivided attention to and it's the same thing with my drawings. That's why I do one portrait at a time because I focus everything on that one thing. Balancing and finding time with friends and family is difficult but the wonderful thing is my true friends and family understand and appreciate that when I do manage to find time to be with them, its quality time we spend with each other. In order to get to where you want to get to in life whether it's professionally, romantically or health-wise is does require you to sacrifice certain things.

Don't Be Discouraged

Try to be wary of the opinions of others especially those that discourage you of your goals or dream particularly if it's one where the intention is to help others. People have such a powerful influence on us and before you know it, the people that you spend time with, you'll end up finding that elements of their character and philosophy of life will have an imprint on you.

In terms of art I would say whatever it is you love to do be true to it and be very careful when being encouraged to follow a successful artist. Find your own unique niche and have the strength and courage in continuing to pursue that.

Second Home

I often take trips to the Tate Modern and Tate Britain and those galleries/museums are my second home. There's so much inspirations there. From understanding what other artists have created and appreciating what they've done and not trying to compare myself with their work, I found myself truly loving what I do and trying to better myself and so in that way I became my own competition.

Priceless Feeling

You can earn an incredible amount of income in this profession but I must stress that it's important to create the work because it's your passion and love, eventually everything else will fall into place and you will be rewarded. In 2009 after finishing university we had an end of year Degree Show and I was working on Trafalgar Square Lions. I sold one of the Lions at the show for £150 but for me at that time, because I had no idea that this was even possible, that £150 felt like a £150,000. It was a priceless feeling for me knowing someone appreciated and invested in my work. As the years went on from honing my skills and believing in my value as an Artist, the demand happened. I feel very fortunate and blessed to be in a position today where a drawing or single portrait of mine will go for £22,000 upwards.

Education

I found my love at a young age for drawing with a pencil, there was an aliveness to it, it was a vehicle for me and I drew without being told. What's completely mind blowing and rewarding for me is that today there are kids who are studying my work as an Artist in contemporary form for GCSE which is truly humbling.

My level of education has enabled me to articulate myself where people can understand what it is I am trying to express or get across. I do believe education is important and understanding the history of art was essential in enabling me not to be naïve or ignorant but in terms of myself as an Artist today, I don't feel it took that much education academically to be able to express myself through the work that I do.

TOP TIPS

1. Understand what it is that you love to do and do it purely because you love to do it.

2. Do your best to preserve regardless of what's happening in your life. Fully believe in yourself and have an unstoppable drive to achieve great results.

3. Lastly, young people should take time to understand and ask themselves 'Who are you as a being?'

THE BLESSINGS OF SOCIAL MEDIA

Social media has definitely played a huge role in my notoriety, recondition and successes as an Artist. Having supporters around the world has put me in a position where I have a platform and whatever I want to say as an Artist or human being, I can share from the heart. From the responses I get, people feel quite inspired when I share stories of my trials, failures and successes of my life and in my art work and appreciate the authenticity of who I am when meeting me in person. This I feel is one of the reasons why I find I have such a strong following.

I WOULD LIKE TO BE REMEMBERED AS...

A being who encouraged others to turn inwards and discover their deeper potential and talents to find that thing that they love to do.

KELVIN OKAFOR PATHWAY PIT STOPS

- Write out a financial statement including what you intend to give in return
- Ask yourself what can you give to life?
- Try to be as present as you can in the moment
- Develop a structure to your day
- Be wary of people who discourage you of your goal/ dream
- Try not to follow a successful Artist. Find your own unique niche.
- Take time to understand and ask yourself 'Who are you as a being?'

KELVIN OKAFOR CONTACT DETAILS

Twitter: @KOkaforart
Instagram: @Kelvinokafor_art
Website: www.kelvinokaforart.com
Email: info@kelvinokaforart.com
Facebook: Kelvin Okafor Art

PAUL THRUSH

Architect

'No man is an island surround yourself with people that can help.'

<u>Paul Thrush Prelude</u>
Paul Thrush is an Architect and co-founder of Stac Architecture which is a young, design-led practice that focuses its energy in the restaurant and bar sector, together with a passion for residential design. Accolades include winning an RABDA (Restaurant and Bar Design Awards) in the fast/casual category for their architecture and design of Nando's Loughton U.K.

PAUL THRUSH INTERVIEW

My name is Paul Thrush I'm an architect by trade but I do interior design work and product design work. I was born and raised in South Africa and studied Architecture there but then I decided to come and see what the western world had to offer and what better place than London where there's a big melting pot of ideas and cultures where the world comes to meet and make things happen.

It's such a great city to make your dreams come true. If you're willing to put in a bit of graft and a bit of work and you know what you want to learn; this city can give you everything.

Differences Between South African and London

In South Africa, for the people and the industry it's about everybody being a jack of all trades. You're expected to know every industry, it's a very 'Yes can do' attitude. Where as in the UK it's very much a 'First World' thing where everything is a lot more specialised.

I sent my CV out when I first got here displaying all my capabilities of being able to do residential work, office work and retail work but I wasn't getting any jobs and then I realised quickly that nobody wants a jack of all trades in London. People want someone who specialises. They don't want someone that can design a car, a chair, a table and a house. It's part of the perception that "You're a jack of all trades, master of none."

To become successful, you need to distinguish yourself

from the rest of the industry and find your own niche.
That's probably the biggest thing I found.

Doing Things A Little Bit Different

I did my Bachelor's degree in Cape Town and Masters in
Port Elizabeth and then I put all the theory into practice
for a year. When you're at university sitting in a lecture
hall surrounded by people, you're just learning things on
paper. But unless you build them you're never going to
know how they work.

I spent a year in Johannesburg and during that summer
I built a church with my own two hands. I found the
obstacles of specialisation were; if you've never had a job
here (in England) no one wants to give you one without
experience. Sending standard CVs and portfolios and
just emailing them out are not going to get noticed. I
started making handmade portfolio's and I personally
delivered them so I could speak to somebody, just doing
things a little bit differently until eventually I got noticed
and got my foot in the door and once you're in there's
no looking back.

It was during the boom years of 2008 when I was
getting paid a good salary to do very little. I would go to
work every day and we'd all sit around these big tables
and every 5 minutes you had someone saying "I'm going
to make a cup of tea would you like one?" You'd draw
something and then talk about your weekend but then
I started to get very frustrated because I studied for 6
years of my life and I was very passionate about what I
did.

Every morning I'd sit on the edge of my bed and would lean down put on my shoes and tie my laces and it was the worst time of the day for me, because once my shoe laces were tied I knew I was out the door going back to the place that I didn't enjoy being at. Then one day I said I can't do this anymore.

I started looking for another job and met an Italian guy who was working by himself in a tiny studio in Islington. He was a creative individual and I really wanted to work for him so I visited his office and delivered my portfolios of work.

He called me back and said "I want you to come and join me but I really can't afford you." I ended up taking a massive pay cut to join but I knew that when I went to join him I'd be doing the things I enjoyed, learning the skills of my trade, being a bit more creative with how design works in London and would basically have fun.

For the next two and half years I enjoyed every single day I went into work. By the time we went our separate ways and I started to do my own thing I had all the experience, portfolio, creativity and the right attitude so it was easy to climb the ladder. It's about self-belief. I knew I had what it takes I just needed that push.

<u>Nando's Recognition</u>
If you're going to become a success to a certain extent you've got to love, breath, sleep your work. Your life, your friends and everything, all forms together to become a success story. If you do that for just one of them the rest just becomes suffocated and kind of die.

My 2 little girls and my marriage are success stories, my business which continues to grow is a success story - the fact that we won Nando's first ever Design Award and it being the first project we ever entered, with loads of designers entering it, we didn't expect to win; that's a success story.

Testing Times

The most trying part of my life was when I was in the process of starting Stac-Architecture and at the same time building my house. I had given in my notice to my previous practice. My wife was pregnant with our second child and was due to give birth in four month's time. I also had some builders on site that were working on my new home and they were ripping the roof off and demolishing the place and I soon realised I employed the wrong people which was very stressful.

Whilst starting this new company I had a contractor at the time which was probably my most nightmare job to date but it was the first one for my own practice and I was trying to figure everything out.

That same week my wife gave birth two months premature which put our little girl in intensive care for more than a month on oxygen and in an incubator.

I had the builders screwing me on one side, the business I'm figuring out on the other, and our little baby in hospital barely holding it together and I just remember one night with my hands in my head thinking what the hell am I going to do.

In the face of all of those things you very quickly realise what's important in life. Number one was my baby girl. Forget about everything else I've got to be at hospital for her as much as she needs me. The second was needing the business to pull through – I'd only just started out and I couldn't afford to have it nose dive now as we wouldn't have money and I've got to make that work. Where there was a sacrifice to be made was my house - we can put that on hold.

What I learnt from all of that is it doesn't matter how many things you're facing. What will ultimately happen is that your priorities will come to the surface. "No man is an island" surround yourself with people that can help.

My friends helped me to build my roof, I had everybody pull together to help me out. You speak to anyone that's been through adversity or far worst and ask whether they've pulled through. It will always sort itself out one way or the other you've just got to get out of bed and make it happen.

Work Ethic & Routines
It's very much more of a team effort as I can't always be creative every day of my life. That's why the employees within our practice are so integral to what we do. I couldn't do it without the people that work with me.

I generally sit with the guys in the office and design. I come up with a game plan for our next big idea or I'm off site to see that next big thing taking shape and coming into action which is really rewarding. The perks about the job is you get to feed your creative mind, you get to travel abroad and meet so many people from other societies and different walks of life and you're not always in the office.

Misconceptions

I think if you ask any man on the street what kind of lifestyle Architects live, they think we're super rich with these big flash modern houses, gorgeous wives/husbands and we walk around with a roll of paper under our arms and drive a Porsche. The reality of it is we're quite underpaid as an industry. We are part of the Arts and part of our downfall is that we like being creative and in order to create you need to put in a lot of time and effort and this costs money and it may not be necessarily right for you.

The pitfall is don't enter this industry if you think you're going to make a shed load of money. If you work for the right companies - big corporate companies and you climb the ladder you can make a name for yourself and make a fair bit of money but it's a slow process. If you want to get into this industry it's got to be for passion, creation and love of design. Only then will you make money as you'll be good at what you do.

A thought to remember is; you don't actually need an architect to build a house. You just need a builder, but an architect will design you a great house. We add value to what we do. People won't hire us because we're a luxury, but if you hire us the end product is worth so much more as we've added value straight back into the project much more so than what our fees actually are.

Education

If I hadn't studied architecture I wouldn't have been an Architect. I don't think it's something you just slip into, but for my situation I would have been a game ranger or still been in South Africa doing other things. However, it's not the education that's made me who I am or made me successful. It's my understanding of people, culture, interpreting briefs, dealing with the client and being personable. Education is one aspect of it. It's definitely a springboard but it's not the be all and end all to everything.

I would say it's important to be a well-rounded individual, who knows what you want and is hungry. In a 'First World' environment, I see a lot of people who aren't hungry. I come from a country where you have to fight for a job, in the UK I feel people become complacent so anybody who is more hungry will overtake you. If you're hungry for food you'll find it, if you're hungry for a job you'll get it. There are so many opportunities in this city and if you are a little bit of savvy, a little bit cheeky, clever and willing to be a bit daring you can go out there and grab it.

TOP TIPS

I don't think everyone knows what they want to be; sometimes you just fall into things you don't have to necessarily know. I think wherever you are in life at the time listen to people, don't necessarily follow them but listen to what they have to say but make your own decisions and carve your own existence. Don't fall into the trap of being like everybody else because then you are in a pocket of society that is very much the same.

I WOULD LIKE TO BE REMEMBERED AS...

It's important for creative people to influence others and it's important that we give something back and that we change the face of the earth. The more people who give the better and memorable the earth will be. So, if I could be just known for sharing, that would be great.

PAUL THRUSH PATHWAY PIT STOP

• Distinguish yourself from the rest of the industry and find your niche
• Realise what's important and make sacrifices
• This industry is for someone who has got passion for creation and love for design
• Education is a springboard but it is not the be all and end all to everything
• Be hungry and don't get complacent
• Listen to what people say but make your own decisions

PAUL THRUSH CONTACT DETAILS

Twitter: @STAC_Paul
Website: www.stac-architecture.com

PAUL A YOUNG

Chocolatier

'Don't count on anyone, be sure of yourself, of your talent and your probity and all will be well.'

<u>Paul A Young Prelude</u>
Paul Young is a ground breaking and inspirational Chocolatier who is at the forefront of the British chocolate scene. Paul's passion for his craft and his cutting edge creativity have won him numerous awards and led him to bring ranked amongst the world's best Chocolatiers.

PAUL YOUNG INTERVIEW

I'm Paul A Young, an award-winning master chocolatier.
I make fresh handmade chocolates daily in my three
London chocolate shops with a team of thirty spread
across my three locations. I have three chocolate recipe
books published including Adventures of Chocolate
which won 'Best chocolate book' in the World at The
Gourmand Cookbook awards.

My Big Break
I started out as a chef and then started to specialise
in the patisserie side. My big break came when Marco
Pierre White offered me a pastry chef position at The
Criterion Brasserie, Piccadilly, London. It was a great
opportunity, one I could not decline and worked for
him for many years in the kitchens of Titanic, The Oak
Room and Quo Vadis. It was tough but working for
Marco taught me to work with a level of detail I had
not experienced before at that time and how to master
perfectionism.

After a career in restaurants I worked as a product
developer for two leaders in retail learning how to
launch a new product from the idea stage to hitting
the shelves. Chocolate took over and I began to
specialise by developing my own style, products and
brand. Breaking into the chocolate market, like any, is
challenging but I thrive on a challenge and it resulted in
an amazing journey. The hours are long of course but
that's the life of any chef especially when it's your own
business and when you are striving to make your mark

within the industry.

There have been many challenges along the way but we've overcome them by having to learn new skills, techniques and for me learning how to manage a growing team and business. I'm passionate about chocolate and that has carried me a long way, but you need something more to succeed. You need a passion that consumes you so that nothing distracts you from your dream.

Grandma's Kitchen

My grandmother and mum were my main role models. I have very fond memories of baking with them in my Grandmother's kitchen every Sunday creating cakes and pies and puddings for all the family. It sparked my passion for food which grew into my career. My mum allowed us to try new foods and to bake and cook from quite an early age. I have a very fond memory of her making the most amazing fudge and toffee, the smell in our tiny kitchen was mesmerising and I wonder if this was the seed planted for my future career.

Chocolate Shop

Opening our first shop was a huge highlight for me. I'd been looking for the right location for years, walking the streets of London, researching and looking at many properties that weren't right, were too expensive, didn't have the right footfall etc. When I found the store on Camden Passage in Islington friends and family helped me to turn a run down and unusable space into a beautiful new chocolate shop, of course I was incredibly proud when it finally opened. It's been a fantastic journey since, we've opened 2 more stores, I've written 3 cookery books, including my latest, Sensational Chocolates in aid of Children's Air Ambulance.

Not My Finest Moment

There are many times when difficulty will hit especially in the early days of your business or new role. I worked relentlessly in the first three years of having the business, it was needed but I failed to acknowledge how tiredness and how stress had made my fuse very short. A chef dropped a tray of truffles and I lost it, screaming and shouting. I had to leave the premises…not my finest moment. A long walk, a phone call to family and a talk with my business partner all put me back on the right track. It was the most difficult time as the business was doing well and I failed to enjoy the fact that we were successful. A tray of dropped chocolates is a small disaster in the grand scheme of things. I apologised to the whole team who were very supportive. Sometimes the hard times snap you back to reality and allow you to step back and view your achievements. This then leads to some seriously strong motivation.

I keep myself motivated by thinking about what can be and what I/we will achieve. Opportunities are endless as are dreams and it's good to dream. It's not at all easy being self-motivated and I at times do need some motivation from my business partner when things get hard. Make sure you have people close to you as you will need them to say the right thing from time to time.

Work Ethic & Routines

No day is the same thankfully as I enjoy the variety of challenges, creativity and excitement... I try and spend time in each of my stores every week both in the shop and in the kitchen working on product development and creating new flavours with my team. I spend a lot of my time with Nicholas my Production Manager developing new products months ahead of time so we can trial the production, shelf life, packaging and costing to ensure it's commercially viable.

A typical week will also consist of one or two interviews with media. We have staff meetings on a regular basis and I liaise with each of the shop managers every day. I receive a large amount of emails which it's important I stay on top of and social media is crucial to promoting the business so I keep that up-to-date.

Nuggets of Time

Finding nuggets of time for myself is now so important. Finding time to feed my creativity is essential and not always easy, one must feed creativity to be able to create. Exercise is really important to me, I have a trainer Davide who helps me find time to exercise, focus and achieve my fitness goals. I eat very well and rarely eat processed food, ready meals or junk food. It's so important to feed your body with the right fuel and in my early days as a chef I failed to do this well.

I love to entertain and cooking for friends is one of my favourite past times. I also love to eat out, it's an inspiration to me to see the latest food trends through the London restaurant scene and a great way to catch-up with friends and family.

Pitfalls to Avoid

Don't go into any catering role whether it's a chef or a chocolatier just because you have seen a chef on TV and it looks glamorous…the food industry can be very glamorous and I LOVED the glamour of the restaurants I have cooked in over the past twenty years and the rewards after years of dedication, blood, sweat and tears can be amazing. I still believe to this day that being a chef is one of the most physically and mentally challenging jobs you can choose to take on. I find it incredibly rewarding of course, it's what drives me on and a love of food in all its forms is what keeps most chefs, cooks and caterers motivated and creative.

Also, pick yourself up from your mistakes; everyone makes them so learn from them so that you're constantly improving.

Quote from a food hero of mine, Antonin Careme:
Advice to young chefs
Young people who love your art;
Have courage, perseverance… Always hope…
Don't count on anyone, be sure of yourself, of your talent and your probity and all will be well.

I've managed to separate myself from the competition by…

Having an intense passion for food and for cacao and chocolate; know your subject well, study, learn the rules then break them again and again so your innovation and intense passion leads you on to rise above your expectations.

I have a 'can do' attitude, say yes to everything, you can always say no later, be a positive person even when things get very hard, I didn't do this well in the beginning but have learned that this will get you further than you can imagine. Smile, motivate and be motivated.

We've separated ourselves from the competition in a number of ways but first and foremost it's a passion for flavour, texture and appearance of my creations. I'm well known for creating unusual flavour combinations, some of which challenge, some make my customers smile and some catch the eye of media which helps keep my business in the public eye. BUT never create a product that's simply a gimmick as you will risk losing your credibility. Sometimes it takes a lot of work to get a flavour combination to work but we always succeed and our customers love it. We never stand still; we're always creating new products.

Self-educate

I went to catering college which gave me a fantastic basis and background education. It taught me all the techniques I needed for entering into a career in food and an appreciation for flavours and ingredients along with a knowledge of how to combine them successfully. Catering college isn't essential for a career in food but it will certainly give anyone an advantage.

You must also self-educate and do endless research so you are the one who stays ahead of the crowd and to feed your inspiration and innovation. Learn a language well as I struggled with French at school but now I use it more often than I ever imagined...a recent trip to French speaking Mauritius as Ambassador of Billington's sugar meant using my limited French skills and a reminder that I should be more language savvy.

TOP TIPS

• Get as much experience as possible, do an apprenticeship, work in a kitchen. This may be daunting, and a frightening thought but do your research and knock on doors not once but many times. A potential employer should be impressed with your perseverance and dedication.

• Keep up-to-date with what's happening in the industry, visit chocolatiers and taste their products, keep an eye on the latest trends and flavours, visit chocolate shows. It demonstrates a passion for working in chocolate.

• Be innovative and be creative – I say this with ease but it's the most challenging skill to implement. Find your own style with influences from your favourite chocolatiers but never directly copy.

I WOULD LIKE TO BE REMEMBERED AS...

I hope that whatever I'm remembered for it includes love and respect.

PAUL A YOUNG PATHWAY PIT STOPS

• Think what could be, what can be and what I/we will achieve
• Everyone makes mistakes so learn from them so that you're constantly improving.
• Have a 'can do' attitude, smile and be motivated.
• Catering college isn't essential for a career in food but it will certainly give anyone an advantage.
• Get as much experience as possible
• Know your subject well, study, learn the rules then break them again and again
• Keep up-to-date with what's happening in the industry
• Find your own style with influences from your favourite chocolatiers but never directly copy.

PAUL A YOUNG CONTACT DETAILS

Twitter: @paul_a_young
Instagram: @paul_a_young
Website: www.paulayoung.co.uk
Facebook: /paulayoungfinechocolates
YouTube: www.youtube.com/c/paulayoung

SHAFIQ HASSAN

Managing Director of Ecko Sourcing
Clothing Manufacturer

'Other people can inspire you but you must inspire yourself.'

Shafiq Hassan Prelude

Shafiq Hassan is the managing Director of Ecko Sourcing in London that supply clothing to global retail chains across Europe. He has also helped to create a foundation called Children's Hope in Dhaka, Bangladesh.

SHAFIQ HASSAN INTERVIEW

My name is Quais Shaifiq ul Hassan and I am the Managing Director of a company called Echo Sourcing in London, as well as Echotex and Shomahar Sweaters both based in Bangladesh. We supply clothing to global retail chains. In London, we have forty employees and in Bangladesh where we do most of our manufacturing, we have over ten thousand people working for our companies.

How I Started Out In My Profession

I studied Industrial Chemistry at City university, London and did a Post Graduate Diploma and Masters in Chemical Engineering at Aston university. Although, I was a mediocre student I somehow managed to get a studentship to do a PhD from the department of Chemical Engineering at Aston. Once I received this opportunity I decided to take a break for a couple years to work in Bangladesh for an NGO, named Brac, which is now the biggest NGO and currently rated the best in the world. Brac's entire focus is on eradicating poverty in a multidisciplinary way. I enjoyed my experience there and wanted to carry on, but Brac's Founder Sir Fazle Hasan Abed suggested that because I have a studentship I should go back and complete my education. Upon my return to the UK and prior to taking on my studentship, I was staying with a friend, who frequently spoke to me about the booming garment industry in Bangladesh, and suggested we set one up ourselves. This option made me sit up and think and for a couple weeks I couldn't get much sleep. I seriously pondered as to whether I should do the PhD or change direction completely to start a garment industry business, in which I was clueless. Having worked for Brac and seeing the work done towards alleviating poverty was truly inspirational I thought that if we did set up a business it could help create employment for poorer women in Bangladesh society, that was also desperately needed. The penny dropped and the course of my life changed.

Pre-teen Role Models
While growing up I had 3 specific pre-teen role models:

My mother Humera Hassan, always taught me, "Never give up". Her education was very basic but she had a lot of wisdom. Throughout my early years, she kept on repeating small verses which became ingrained in me. A particular phrase that always stands out is "Never say you can't do anything, if you can't do it ninety-nine times, try the hundredth time!" One never knows what we take in subliminally.

My father Obiadul Hassan, had an unbelievable influence on me. He was a successful dentist and in his lifetime, there were significant things I learnt that had a profound effect on me. Throughout my childhood, he showed me the value of giving, taking care of people, hard work, integrity, independence and doing things on time. For twenty years, he voluntarily worked 3 days a week for a nominal fee at a government hospital serving poor people. I remember visiting him on my weekends and there used to be a couple of hundred people each day that he would take care of. I also learned from his life and work the importance of giving without expecting anything back.

My uncle, (my father's youngest brother) Sayeedul Hassan, had a career as a diplomat, successful at business and a political leader of a party that represented the poor, industrial workers and peasants. He was a remarkable human being as he gave so much care to all who met him and the love that he gave us is unforgettable. During the liberation war of Bangladesh in 1971, his best friend and also one of the most influential Hindu's in then, East Pakistan took shelter at his home in the capital Dhaka. My uncle a Muslim, was aware of the risk he was taking, because the Pakistani Army were specifically tasked to annihilate Hindus from East Pakistan. The Pakistani Army found out about this situation, took them both and murdered them. This taught me the meaning of ultimate courage and sacrifice.

Biggest Success to Date

On a personal level, my biggest success has been being able to give quality time to some key people in my life. Time is the most precious thing in anyone's life and so I try my best to share time with those I hold dearest.

In terms of work, my success is being able to share this journey with my partner Para Hamilton; we've been friends and business partners for the best part of thirty years. She's been a great influence and my muse. We had the common goal of doing things for the right reasons. Whatever we did in business we always thought about the welfare of the people who are working with/for us, the people in our team whether they are our workers in our factories, offices, designers or in management, we regard them to be the most important aspect of our work.

I believe that luck is the people that you meet who become part of your journey, and as a team you achieve whatever you do.

In Bangladesh, we created a foundation called Children's Hope in 2000, that works with children and their families in Dhaka slums for both those with ability and disability. We have worked with several hundred children and over a hundred have graduated from Universities. I believe that education is one of the key factors to break the cycle of poverty among the poorest of societies, so Children's Hope provides this opportunity and much more. It was very satisfying to have set up this organisation when we first saved some funds for the company and along the way other companies and individuals have also contributed to this cause, both locally and internationally.

Necessity is the Mother of Invention

Throughout anything that you do, you have to face obstacles and overcome them to succeed. Adversity comes in many different forms and nothing in life is smooth. Two years after the formation of our company, in 1998 a challenge came from our main competitor, Greece. Greek companies had a delivery time of 4 weeks after receiving an order and ours from Bangladesh was fourteen weeks. Although Greece was much faster than us, they were also much more expensive than us for a like for like product. Our main customer *New Look* Retailers Ltd advised us that if we couldn't significantly reduce our delivery lead time then there would be no business. As necessity is the mother of invention we had to come up with something to survive.

We had to innovate and work out as to how we would reduce delivery from 14 weeks to 4 or less to compete with Greece. Para went to Greece on a fact-finding mission, and I travelled to Bangladesh, spent several weeks speaking to our team and key suppliers and came up with a solution as to how we could make stuff within 2 weeks, bring goods by air and deliver within the 4-week period, which enabled us to not only equal Greece but also to do it better, cheaper and faster! What we achieved was some sort of a revolution, as this was unheard of then and when I relate this story to others now, people think it's very difficult even now, but impossible then. We made it happen and business grew from £1.5m to £20m in five years! We had to take a challenge and make it into an opportunity, an important aspect to any business. Some regard that we pioneered fast fashion in the Bangladesh garment industry.

Pitfalls to Avoid

The earlier you decide what you enjoy doing is what is going to give you the most returns, not necessary always monetarily. If you can help it, you shouldn't do something for the sake of doing it, you should do it because you believe in it. That way you get so much more out of it. I think lot of people suffer pitfalls because they don't share their thoughts with others properly. Everyone should be able to find one or two people that they can bounce their ideas off. You make up your own mind but if you can find a couple of people who you can trust to listen to you and help to clear your thoughts, it will enable you to make better decisions and make less mistakes.

Nothing Happens Overnight

I want to stress to young people that there is no substitute for hard work. It's really critical to know that whether you run a business or work for a company, nothing happens overnight. To be ahead of competition you've got to think out of the box, be innovative, consistently think about doing things differently and have your own niche/signature. That comes through by thinking about what you do, how you do it and evaluating yourself on a continuous basis. Once you challenge yourself and do what you believe in, it automatically influences other people. Have a vision, perform to a level that is world class and push yourself to be the best.

Prove Your Worth!

I would advise young people not to think about money too much. Never judge anything by how much you earn. Money is important and we need money to live but if you do well, prove your worth and ability in anything that you do well in, money shall come to you, but above all your satisfaction is priceless. If you put your heart and mind for example into being a successful designer and consistently develop your skills over a number of years you can earn a 6-figure salary, who knows, you could also have your own brand!

Education

Education is not everything but it has definitely given me grounding to be organised and think from different angles, and at university I learnt so much from people of different backgrounds and cultures that made me a fuller person. Also, I think my engineering background helped me to grapple with complex ideas and possibly understand processes quicker.

TOP TIPS

Try and think out of the box; think of new things and have a vision. Other people can inspire you but you must also inspire yourself from within and the key part I think is to believe in yourself.

Hard work is absolutely a pinnacle; The Beatles were together for over 10 years, working hours and hours, before they had their first hit single. There are thousands of paintings by Picasso that are in a vault in Paris that have never seen the light of day. The hard work that he must have put in to become a master is unthinkable but no one sees that. We only see the end result, which in both cases is greatness.

Gather Experience; It's a good idea to gain 3-4 years' experience with different companies to help you grow and learn.

Building a team; nothing can be done without people, they are everything. Building a team is vitally important for running a successful business.

I WOULD LIKE TO BE REMEMBERED AS...

Someone that gave the best for the people that are close to me, and what I leave behind can help inspire people and make a positive difference.

SHAFIQ HASSAN PATHWAY PIT STOPS

• Never give up
• Have friends you can bounce ideas off
• Have a vision, perform to a level that is world class and think out of the box
• Hard work is absolutely pinnacle
• Gather experience by working for different companies
• Build a team; people are everything

SHAFIQ HASSAN CONTACT DETAILS

Website: www.echosourcing.com

CHRISTINE HODGSON

Chairman of Capgemini UK
Digital Technology

'Be curious and have an enquiring mind.'

Christine Hodgson Prelude
Christine Hodgson is Chairman of Capgemini UK plc.
She also chairs the Capgemini Group Sustainability
Board and the UK Women's Business Network.
Christine has worked at Capgemini for nineteen years in
a number of UK and Global roles.

CHRISTINE HODGSON INTERVIEW

My name is Christine Hodgson; I am the Chairman of Capgemini in the UK. Capgemini is a technology services company and my background is a chartered accountant by profession. I have been with the company for nearly nineteen years.

From Accountancy and Beyond

I started out as an accountant, I did a four-year accountancy degree (it was a sandwich degree) and in my third year I went to work for a big accountancy firm Coopers & Lybrand. Once I graduated I went back to work for them and did more exams as a chartered accountant and after staying there for a few years I joined one of my clients at Ronson Plc. I worked there for nearly 5 years before I came to work at Capgemini.

I don't think I have actually had many obstacles in my career. I've had setbacks and things not go particularly well but my experiences are that you actually learn more from those difficult situations than you do from when everything's going swimmingly well.

When I was at Ronson's I fell in love with the boss which wasn't a good thing to do and I wouldn't recommend that, then separate to that during my time there we had a fire that nearly killed the company off. I was the Finance Director and I was trying to work out whether we had enough money to pay the suppliers and it was a really tense time, all of which ultimately made me stronger.

My Parents

I can't honestly remember there being a role model other than my parents. They were the people I looked up to the most. I was the youngest of four older siblings and came from a very happy and secure family background that made me feel like I could do anything.

I knew from an early age that I wanted to work hard and do the best I possibly could to please them. My parents were very encouraging in a non-pressuring way and so whenever I did anything that I was proud of I always wanted to tell my mum and dad before I told anyone else. Their nearly ninety years old and I still feel like that now.

Capgemini/Careers and Enterprise Company

My biggest success apart from my 9 year old son who is everything to me, I would say getting to where I am today. It has taken me many, many years and I'm most proud of the things that I'm doing at Capgemini having helped transform the business. An initiative I currently champion is an evening job I do for the Government where I chair the Careers and Enterprise Company which is all about joining up businesses and schools in a way that's more impactful for young people. What we try to do is connect businesses and schools and try to show young people the sort of skills they need for the future and demystify the world of work and hopefully help them to see loads of different opportunities. One of the things the government has asked us to create is an Enterprise Passport – a digital record of all the things young people do aside from their academic results. The hope is that in time the employer will say "Show me your passport" and it will be on a colour coded record of snaps of everything they've done/achieved.

Bouncing Back

The time I felt most adversity was when I was working at Ronsons Plc. After the fire, we had gone from being quite a rich company to suddenly having no money as our stock went up in flames. The banks who lent us money wanted their money back and eventually I lost my job after 5 years. The adversity was being unemployed as up to that point I had always had a job and all of a sudden, my motivation was to get back into employment very quickly. I found it very disconcerting as I was professionally qualified and everything had been going all in one direction and suddenly everything was not so easy anymore. When I look back to that period of time it was definitely the best learning experience of my life. It's the only time I've felt real stress in a work environment and so when I came to Capgemini everything felt so much more straight forward.

Finding a Balance

I wake at 6am in the morning and I get my son ready for school as he has a long commute. I leave home at 7am to get to the office for 7.30am and I will work until 6pm. I then desperately dash home so I can see my son and encourage him to do his homework and read to him before he goes to bed. Afterwards I may do some extra work at night from home or I may have a client dinner. Throughout Monday to Friday my days are absolutely chock-a-block. My work ethic is full on but where I try to keep a bit of balance is by not working on weekends and taking all my holiday leave. I think for me being a working mum that is essential because it's when I get to spend real quality time with my son.

As a Chairman, I'm not somebody who wants everybody to stay in the office late at night. I really don't think that's healthy, I think if people are doing that consistently it probably means they're either out of control or we've not got the right resources on the job. We'll always have projects that have deadlines, they'll always be peaks but if there's peaks all the time then there is something fundamentally wrong. One of the things about having a young child is that it makes you very conscious of your own productivity. I am believer in that you should measure success on output not the number of hours that you work. There's not much that's healthy and balanced about my lifestyle but I manage it in the best way I know how. When it comes to friends and family I try to see them as much as I can on the weekends.

Pitfalls To Avoid

I wouldn't characterise it necessarily to my profession but I would just say generally that a pitfall people have is that they can be very ambitious (and there's nothing wrong in that) but if the ambition is too blinding sometimes they can get ahead of themselves. One piece of advice I'd share which is something I read from Sir Roger Carr (current Chairman at BAE Systems) "If you do the current job well the next job will take care of itself" and I really believe that. If you do a good job and then put your hand up and say "I can do more" people will start to see that you can take on more and you can do it. Whereas if you trying to get 3 steps ahead before you've proved that you can do the first step then you're quite likely to fall on your face. Rather than getting caught in that trap just do a really good job in everything that you're given to do and along the way you'll be given opportunities which will then allow you to determine your own future success.

Attributes Needed To Be Successful

I would say the attributes that I've found useful are my interpersonal skills - building and investing in relationships, being interested in people I work with - suppliers, partners, clients, client's businesses and the economy. Relationships are all about something that is nurtured over a very long period of time that pay dividends for you and for them. Resilience – you can't be precious when you're in a position like mine. If you're too sensitive, you'll wither and die quite quickly. So be curious and have an enquiring mind. I've always worked hard and put my back into everything that I do as I'm driven by never wanting to let anybody down in whatever I'm doing.

Capgemini Apprenticeships

Education has been very important for me because I went down a very traditional route. From school, I went to university, from university I did a chartered accountancy and so for me it's been a very structured pathway. I don't think it has to be like that, take Richard Branson for example, he didn't go to university. Entrepreneurs go down entrepreneurial routes. One of the most exciting things I think for young people is apprenticeship schemes. At Capgemini, we offer one hundred apprenticeships a year for young people aged eighteen. They don't pay any tuition fees as we are linked with Aston university and upon graduating they will have a combination of 5 years' work experience/on the job training, a degree and a job at Capgemini if they want to stay on and work with us. The younger people can start building experiences of work through volunteering and other means as early as they can, eventually employers won't ask "What GSCE's did you get?" What they'll ask is "What do you do in your spare time?" So, they can get a picture of you as a citizen rather than somebody who can or can't sit exams.

TOP TIPS

I would say get as many professional type qualifications as you can, not everybody likes taking exams and that's fine but you can get experience and it is about trying to demonstrate levels of competence.

My second tip would be to aim high but go through the steps – don't feel as though there's any sort of ceiling you're going to reach because I think anybody can go a long way but there is no substitute for hard work.

Thirdly, I would say take a few risks. Sometimes when you're in a job or something that feels quite cosy you think "I'll just stay doing this" but actually you tend to learn from doing different things.

Looking back at my career when I was a Finance Director and somebody had said I could go and be the Chief Executive for the company in Europe - you think "Crikey can I do that?! What happens if I can't do it? What happens if I fail?" But take a calculated risk, say "I'll do it", learn as you go and you'll become stronger and grow as a result from that.

Live/Work Abroad!

The one thing that I have never done that I would have liked to have done is to live abroad. I came close a couple of times, firstly to live in Hong Kong while I was with Coopers & Lybrand and secondly with Capgemini when I was Finance Director of the Global Outsourcing Business. There was a period when the Boss and I were going to base ourselves in Mumbai, India and we got as far as finding the apartments where we were going to stay and then I was offered the job of being the Chief Executive of Europe and so that was the end of that. But I do think you get a very rich experience listening to people who've done it - Not just learning the language but culturally too. So, if you're lucky enough to work for a company that can give you those opportunities then I would say grab them.

Closing Thoughts

Without sounding cheesy I guess anyone who runs a company would like to be remembered as an inspirational leader so I hope that people would have enjoyed working for me and I would have done something to inspire them.

CHRISTINE HODGSON PATHWAY PIT STOP

• Aim high but go through the steps
• If you do the current job well, the next job takes care of itself
• Build and invest in your relationship with people
• Look into apprenticeships schemes with Capgemini
• Take calculated risks
• If you're lucky enough to have the opportunity to work abroad take it

CHRISTINE HODGSTON CONTACT DETAILS

Website: www.uk.capgemini.com

DANNY RICHMAN

Entrepreneur

'I learned a lot just by opening myself up to as many experiences as possible.'

<u>Danny Richman Prelude</u>

Danny Richman is an Entrepreneur and SEO consultant with over twenty years' experience. His clients include BBC, Bank of England and the John Lewis Partnership.

DANNY RICHMAN INTERVIEW

My name is Danny Richman; I am an entrepreneur and have been running my own businesses for nearly thirty-three years.

My Million Pound Software Idea

I left school shortly after my sixteenth birthday with no idea as to what I was going to do. I went through my school days with my teachers telling me I was stupid, lazy and that I would never amount to anything. Somehow, I managed to get a part time job in a curtain shop where customers would choose the fabric they would like for their curtains. They would come in with all of their window measurements and then ask how much it would cost to get them made up.

Working out the cost of making curtains was quite a big problem. You had to calculate how much fabric would be needed, the lining, the heading tape and all of the making costs etc. The only person who knew how to do this was the shop owner, Harry.

Around this time, the first-ever home computer came out in the U.K (The Sinclair ZX81) which cost £100 and came with a book on how to write your own computer program. A friend of mine was given one of these as a birthday present, took one look at it and thought it was just geeky nonsense.

He showed it to me when I went to his house and I thought it looked pretty cool. My friend said "If you want it you can have it." So, I took it home, and this computer and I got on like a house on fire.

I learnt how to develop programs and really wanted to start doing something useful with it. So, I went to see my boss, Harry at the curtain shop and asked him to show me how to work out costings for curtains so that I could try to write a program that will do that job. After eight months, I had a working program which all of the staff were able to use and give customers curtain quotations.

It was the first time in my life I had done something that I felt proud of. My boss, Harry told other people in the industry about the computer software I'd developed. He encouraged me to set up a business and attend an annual trade exhibition called 'Home Interiors'.

The event lasted three days. The only thing I had brought with me was my computer with the software installed on it. I estimated that I might sell 10 computers so decided to charge £275 (£100 for the computer and £175 for my software). I gave demonstrations of how it works to potential customers. I said that if they wanted to buy it they could pay me and I would then order it for them. By the close of day three I had sold just under 4,000 machines and taken payments of over a million pounds. That's the crazy story of how I got started in business.

I used that same concept for the next fifthteen years and just adapted the software for different industries such as carpets, car repairs, double-glazing and building quotations. I eventually sold the business to a much larger company.

Role Model Father

I would have to say my dad was my role model growing up. He had been involved in running his own business for many years. I learned a lot through watching him and seeing what he did. When I finished the 'Home Interiors' exhibition the best part was when my dad told me he was proud of me for the first time in my life. Whatever age you are, when your parents say they are proud of you, it's very important and means a lot.

Prince's Trust

The work I do at the Prince's Trust probably gives me the most satisfaction. I work with around five hundred young people at the Trust every year. They really inspire me, especially those that have come from difficult backgrounds and upbringings. To see them connect with something and overcome the barriers that they've had in their life is really inspiring to watch. If there is anything I've done to help those people that makes me feel good. I consider that work to be my biggest success.

Finding What Makes Me Happy

When your business is financially successful you may think that your problems are over. Actually, this was the most difficult period for me and I became unhappy with my life and with what I was doing.

I felt quite depressed around my mid- thirties and there

was a real danger I was going to destroy this great business I had created because I felt so unmotivated. The key thing for me in overcoming this was really about just focusing on my biggest priorities in life.

I had spent such a long time growing the business and being so driven to making more and more money that I had completely lost touch with myself. I realised, after fifthteen years, that money wasn't the thing making me happy. So I had to sit down and ask myself "What does make me happy?". I couldn't answer this question. All I did know was that carrying on doing what I was doing wasn't the answer.

So, I made a decision that I was going to stop running the business and just say "yes" to any new opportunity that came my way (unless I had a really good reason to say no). So, I went off and did some acting, played music, got involved in all sorts of activities; working with different charities and homeless groups to try to understand myself better and help me connect with what made me happy.

I learned a lot just by opening myself up to as many experiences as possible. I learned about both the things I like doing and don't like doing. I now spend much more time doing the things I enjoy. Without doubt, that was the best decision I ever made. I'm now very strict with myself about making sure that I'm involved in work that makes me feel happy and fulfilled, whether that makes money or not.

Work Ethic & Routines

If it wasn't for my wife I'd probably be working all the time. She's really good at making sure that we spend lots of time together seeing friends and family, taking long walks in the country and going on holidays.

I don't really have a fixed daily routine because I now do so many different things. Sometimes I'll be working from home, dealing with phone calls, answering emails, doing work on the computer etc. A couple of days a week I am working with young people at the Prince's Trust. On other days, I go to client meetings around London or meeting people in their offices. I must be one of Uber's best customers!

Pitfalls to Avoid

A common thing I find working with young people at the Prince's Trust who are starting a business is that they think a lot about what they like and what they want to do. What they forget sometimes is that, whatever business you're in, it's probably not going to work unless you're actually solving somebody's problem. There a business term called "Product Market Fit". It's really just about making sure there's a strong demand for your product or service, a real need for what you're doing and that people will be willing to pay for it. Everything else is just the icing on the cake.

Also, when you're starting out in business a lot of people think that their biggest problems are going to be external factors like competition, finding customers or understanding their target market. I actually find that the biggest challenges people usually face are internal challenges – elements where they lack knowledge, confidence or find it difficult to have a working relationship with other people. The first challenge is always to work on yourself.

Attributes Needed to be Successful

When you're starting out in business, you're going to be doing a lot of different jobs. You're going to need to know about marketing and have a good understanding of finances and cash-flow etc. So, you have to be willing to learn about lots of different things.

There will often be a few lean years. This is typical before you are generating enough income to pay yourself a liveable salary. However, once it's off the ground, and depending on how ambitious you are and how good your business is, there's really no limit to how much you could make.

One quality that has served me well over the years working in technology is that I find I am able to communicate technical concepts in simple layman's terms using language that people understand and I feel that this has helped enable me to stand out from my competition.

Education

I didn't really have much of a secondary school education at all. I just didn't engage there. It really wasn't a good school and I wasn't a good student. All of my education has come since I left school. If there's one message I would like to give to younger people who are struggling at school; I would say, all is not lost. Education doesn't have to be in a school or a classroom. There are so many ways you can learn by yourself and broaden your knowledge, especially now with the internet. The world's knowledge is all there, right at your fingertips!

Be Open to Opportunities

My dad used to tell me a fictional story about a man who was stranded at sea and washed up on a desert island in the middle of the ocean. There was no food, no water, nothing; he just lay on this island, dying.

The man said to himself, "I'm not worried because I believe in God and God is going to save me". Four days later, in the distance, he sees a ship. They call to him from the ship and ask "Are you OK?" The man says "I'm fine". They ask, "Do you want us to pick you up and save you?" He replies "No, I have faith in God, God will save me" and so the ship moves on.

A couple of days later a helicopter comes along and they call down to the man and ask, "Do you want us to save you?" He again says "No. God will save me". Three days later he dies and goes to heaven. He sees God in heaven and says, "God I've got a bone to pick with you! I put all my faith in you and I still died and you didn't save me!" God says to the man, "What are you talking about? I sent you a ship and a helicopter!"

For me, this is a great lesson in understanding that you need to be open to opportunities. All of us have some opportunities that come our way if we are in the right state of mind to see them and then act on them. Luck definitely helps, but a positive mental attitude beats luck any day.

TOP TIPS

Firstly, find a problem that needs solving. A good entrepreneur is someone who identifies problems, sees the opportunities then does something about it. Lots of people have good ideas but then never actually do anything about it.

Second tip, is don't try and do everything alone. It's so much harder to operate as an island. Things become so much easier if you share your experiences, network with other people and try to meet other people who are going through the same thing as you.

Thirdly, do something that gives you enjoyment and fulfilment. If you do something just for the financial reward, I'm not convinced it's going to work in the long term.

I WOULD LIKE TO BE REMEMBERED AS...

Somebody who was always curious about how the world works and driven to understand it better. My interests range from technology to psychology to neuroscience to economics and to culture. I am always hungry to learn more. I hope that curiosity stays with me until my last days on Earth.

DANNY RICHMAN PATHWAY PIT STOP

- Product/Market Fit; Your business idea must help to solve somebody's problem
- Continue to work on yourself; Education doesn't have to be in a school or a classroom
- Don't try to do everything alone
- Do something that gives you enjoyment and fulfilment
- Be open to opportunities; Luck definitely helps, but a positive mental attitude beats luck any day.

DANNY RICHMAN CONTACT DETAILS

Website: www.seotraininglondon.org
LinkedIn: uk.linkedin.com/in/dannyrichman

SIMON GREEN

Events Planner/Tour Manager

'Nothing good comes easy - Climbing Mount Everest is hard but people still do it.'

Simon Green Prelude
Simon Green is an experienced tour and production manager who has worked with major global artist touring the UK, Europe and World Wide including Wu Tang Clan, Pusha T, Maya Jane Coles, Paigey Cakey, Duke Dumont, William Singe, Hammer, Ty, Lethal Bizzle and many more.

SIMON GREEN INTERVIEW

My name is Simon Green I am a Production and Tour Manager and I run a small Events Company.

In The Early Days
When I started my career in the creative industries I had just come out of a traumatic experience after I was wrongfully sacked having worked as a Fire fighter for twenty years. Even though I ended up winning my case in court, the immediate impact of not having a job had a devastating effect on my circumstances during that period of time as I had a mortgage to pay and was raising a young family with no work and no income. It was then that I decided that I needed to do a job that I enjoyed. There's an old cliché of "If you enjoy doing a job you love then it's not really a job." I've been interested in music all my life and felt that I wanted to give something back so after discussing things over with my wife and working out the finances of how much I needed to earn each month she gave her blessing and provided me with the space to do my thing, to take risks and develop. So, I started out by doing amateur things such as DJing and Events Production and tried to turn that into a living and as the months went by I began to make enough money to make ends meet.

Big Up the Teachers
My first role models were my teachers; even though I'm working class and went to a really rough comprehensive school I was considered to be quite clever by my teachers which was lucky for me. I got into some areas

that most of the estate guys wouldn't such as theatre groups, school orchestra and poetry. Some of my teachers even lent me their records. They really believed in me and went out of their way to support me, show me direction, guidance and opportunity.

Touring with Wu Tang Clan

Being a Production Manager I've done some massive events such as Love Music, Hate Racism, Festival stages at Glastonbury, The Big Chill and so on.

One day a friend of mine called Ty – A legendary South London Rapper needed a Tour Manager but he didn't have much budget. I offered to help him out as my diary was empty. This was my first time taking on a role like this but I guess what helped me was that I was familiar with what a Tour Manager does as I was engaging with them all the time throughout other projects I had worked on as a Production Manager.

Ty's tour turned out to be fantastic and months later he invited me on the next one he had lined up in Germany, Belgium and France. I soon began to find that I loved the travelling, adventure and problem solving of Tour Managing and the fact that it's different every day.

The word spread around town that I'm a bit of a Tour Manager as unbeknown to me, Ty is telling the world that "I'm very good" and so naturally my phone started to ring - and as Ty is a legend in UK Hip Hop this eventually opened doors for me to work with the Wu-Tang Clan.

An agent that I know was having a conversation in New York with Devine (Manager of Wu Tang Clan.) Devine was fed up with the hiring, firing and burn out of Tour Managers as the Wu Tang Clan are quite a challenging band to work with. He needed someone who could handle the band and grow with them because there were some big future projects coming up and so the agent said "You need to phone Simon Green, he's your guy." So randomly out of the blue I get a call from Devine and he asked me if I was interested in the project and within half a second I said "Yes!" because I realised what a massive opportunity this was.

So, I believe my greatest achievement in this industry is that I was the Tour Manager and part of the Production Management team for Wu Tang Clan, an A-level band that performed in front of audiences of up to seventy thousand people each night for their Twentieth Anniversary Tour around the world which was truly amazing.

Tackling Adversity Head On

I firmly believe in going forward inch by inch and that's why I love the job that I do. Nothing good comes easy - Climbing Mount Everest is hard but people still do it. For some people projects or creative projects from a management point of view can be a series of difficulties but from my perspective it's a series of creative challenges and so I'm problem solving all the time. I face adversity everyday – planning is important but sometimes the plan can go wrong and the question is how do you get through the adversity when it arrives in front of you? You're in front of a wall and you can't get through. Do you go over? Do you go under? Do you go around the side? Do you kick the wall down…? How do you go forward? The most important thing to remember is that a wall is not going to stop you. Somehow, you're going to leave it behind and get through it. You can't just crumble, start sucking your thumb and curl into a ball and tuck yourself under a blanket. At that point the pressures on and you have to rise to the challenge.

Work Ethic & Routines

In my industry, (depending on what I am doing) a day is long and so I can work up to fourteen hours or longer which is not unusual. From the time I get up I would have pre-planned the night before what's going happen so I'm ready for it or at least thought it through. So, I wake up early make sure I get some food and then I grind, getting through a list of tasks on my schedule from flight arrangements and where the Tour Bus will be parked, all the way through to sound checking. So, I'll be walking the event through in my head each step of the way and that's my opportunity to check I haven't forgotten anything and that I have everything covered or that I've developed a plan B scenario as a precaution.

In my role, the 3 steps I cover are; The Advance, The Delivery and the Post Production which essentially are the before, during and after stages of an event. Planning is the hidden part of what I do and most artists don't realise the massive amount of pre-planning that can go into a show.

How I balance It All Out

My industry isn't clock in at 8am and finish at 5pm. If I wanted that lifestyle I would drive a truck or work in a factory. What I do have however is a fully supportive and very understanding Wife. So, when I say I have to go to Paris tomorrow for 3 days she's not moaning or cussing me out. I get to go with her full blessing. In Europe and all around the world, festival season is during the summer time and so from May through to September my diary is mainly wiped out. When I come back home from tour dates we get our family time and do family stuff together with the kids too.

Don't Be Deterred

The most difficult part is entering this profession. That is where the walls are highest and where the doors are closed especially for disadvantaged young people. The creative industries can be very privileged.

The fact that now there are more young people entering the industry shows that you guys have beaten down some of that stuff. So, my advice would be don't be deterred. As a young person if you've got no skills you have no value. So, you need to attach yourself to a project where you can see how it works, understand the processes and build up your skill set. The pitfalls to avoid are wasting time, money and energy. Make time to engage and rise in the industry, maintain enough energy to grind and keep going, and try to spend less money than you earn.

Separating Myself from The Competition

I do that by taking every project as it comes, learning how to manage challenging artists, being able to work effectively and professionally with people and understanding various job roles within my industry. I'm a freelancer so depending on the size and scale of a project you sometimes need help and having a team is so important - everyone is a cog. I have this thing about staying in your lane. I'm not a publisher but I know a bit about publishing, I don't work for a record label but I know a bit about record labels, I'm not a promoter but I know a bit about promoting. I'm a tour manager/ production manager and in this area, I know my stuff and not many can compete with me.

How to Earn a Salary

The industry is currently in a financial turmoil. I'm not going to lie things are hard. For my particular job role, the range of fees varies. At a low level (when I say low I mean the artists aren't making a lot of money) it would be from £0 - £100 a day, an average fee £150 - £250 a day and the very top level £1,000 a day are the going rates. The higher the fees your artist is earning the more money you'll get. You could earn £1,000 a day but if you only work one day of the year it's not so great. So, the trick is not the day rate but trying to get twenty shows a month. That's how you will earn an annual salary.

Education

I got here by being extremely good at what I do and putting myself in a position where I am the 'First Call' for anyone requiring my services. The opportunity of working with Wu Tang Clan was like my university education in this job role. I don't have a degree but most people I sit in a room with to discuss projects and ventures do have degrees. Generally, the topic of education is never brought up and what people do respect me for is the value I bring and the experience I've got.

What I would say to young people is university is a pathway that can help you get experience and gain broader knowledge of the industry and it's the same with internships or work placement opportunities with particular firms. However, even more important is that you have to be willing to put in the hard graft and develop working relationships with people.

Triangle of Success

The secret to being the 'First Call' as a freelancer is 3 magic things which I call the triangle of success.

1. Be professional – Be on time for meetings, have your address book and contacts up to date. Use the language of the industry. You're not born professional but you're learning the industry every hour of every day.

2. Come in on a fair price – What is your value? What are you bringing to the project? What is a fair price? You can come in too cheap or too expensive, try and come in fair.

3. Never miss a deadline – The whole of the creative industries works on deadlines. When a project has a lot

of people working together on it, it's not just you who's late and messes up. Missing a deadline will generate a domino effect which then generally leads to something bad happening.

If you can stick to these 3 key principles I promise you your phone will ring. That's how you build and your snowball grows bigger and bigger. Seriously. It's that easy.

The World's my Oyster
I currently work as Pusha T's Tour Manager and have done so for the past 3 years as well as doing other projects that fall under Kanye West's Good Music record label. Working with them is a privilege as they are really creative and great people to be around. I'm having a fantastic time and nothing gets better than this so I'm very content in what I'm doing. I'm also working on a few other projects with Wu-Tang Clan and other artists. I love my role in this industry.

I WOULD LIKE TO BE REMEMBERED AS...

A man who was exceptional at his job, who gave back and helped people to climb the ladder of success.

SIMON GREEN PATHWAY PIT STOP

• If you enjoy doing job a job you love, then it's not really a job
• Make a checklist of tasks that need doing
• Don't be deterred
• Attach yourself to projects to build up your skillset

- Try to spend less money than you earn
- Put yourself in a position to be the 'First Call'
- Use the Triangle of Success

SIMON GREEN CONTACT DETAILS

Twitter: @headancer
Instagram: @simon_green
LinkedIn: uk.linkedin.com/in/simonpetergreen

DANIELLE CARTER

Footballer

'Put the work in now and you're going to set yourself up for a better life.'

Danielle Carter Prelude

Danielle Carter is a WSL professional Footballer for Arsenal Women FC and the England national team. Her accolades include scoring a hat trick on her senior debut for England as well as scoring the winning goal in the 2016 FA Cup final for Arsenal Women FC.

DANIELLE CARTER INTERVIEW

My name is Danielle Carter, I'm an Arsenal FC and England Footballer and graduated from university with a Physiotherapy Degree.

Rising Through The Ranks
I started off at Leyton Orient's Sunday team and then that progressed to the centre of excellence which was my Saturday league. I was there until I was 16 years old and then I moved straight to Arsenal and am now entering my 8th season with them.

Role Models
My mum is my role model. She's done so much for me. She travelled everywhere with me. Without her support I wouldn't be where I am today. Rachel Yankey, who I've had the honour of playing with at Arsenal Women FC for 7 years was someone I looked up to growing up so to have that experience of actually playing in the same team as her is great.

First Senior Cap
I would say representing England for the first time and getting that first senior cap was one of my greatest achievements. I scored a hat-trick on my debut and then followed that up with another hat-trick in my next appearance. It's not an official record (The Guinness Book of Records haven't come to me yet!) but I don't think anybody's actually done that before. It's something I'm really proud of.

Outside of Football it would be my degree. I struggled massively with that from the first year. Once I was able to graduate, and having my family there to witness that achievement was a proud day I'll never forget. Still to this day I look back and I don't know how I completed it. It was tough, training all the time and then having to go into lectures, especially with the course I was on, where I had to be there every day until 5pm.

FA Cup Final 2016
This was an amazing day! To be able to play at Wembley alone was a dream come true, but to then go and score the winning goal there was unbelievable! We won the FA Cup for a record fourteenth time. I had a good seventy plus friends and family who came to watch me that day so was nice for them to witness this.

Training and Match days
The beginning of pre-season is built a lot on physical based stuff to get you up to speed. During the season, generally we'll train 4-5 times a week with 1 or 2 days off. At times, there could be double training, so we'll have a football based session out on the pitch then we'll go in the gym the same day to do another workout. Leading up to the games we focus on what we'll do tactically to get ready for the match on Sunday. The best part of it all is playing and to be able to get out there and do what you love. It's a fantastic feeling.

Put Your Prioritises In Order
It's easy to say but try to be mature. Obviously, you're not really mature at fourteen/fifthteen but don't be

easily led or follow peer pressure or people that you think are cool. Try and think outside the box. Know where you want to end up. Just think "Put the work in now and you're going to set yourself up for a better life."

I think from a young age this has been put into practice whereby when my friends go out some nights and I can't because I've got a game the next day. It's something that I've grown up with in a sense and now it's second nature. I know how to prioritise what needs to be done and what can wait. I can go out anytime but my career is ultimately the most important thing so I can miss a party or two.

Do That Little Bit Extra

If you're with a team and you're training twice a week, you can do other things around that. Maybe one day go for a run or go to the park and have a kick about, keep on top of your skills and keep trying to develop little things that you might need to improve on because every little counts. It might not seem like your progressing but over time you'll realise it all starts to click into place and you'll appreciate the effort you've put into that.

Luckily, I've never really faced significant adversity. I've had set backs in terms of not being selected to play certain games or I don't get to go on certain trips but that just pushes me to work harder so that I am there the next time or that when I get the opportunity I am ready and not playing catch up.

Attributes Needed to be A Successful Footballer

Dedication and commitment. Diligence is a big one; when no one's watching, what are you actually doing? It might not look pretty but behind closed doors what is it that you're doing to keep up and improve yourself on a daily basis. Whether it be nutrition wise or lifestyle, all those things add up so you have to be diligent in that sense.

Have a Plan B

I was always a bit of a maths geek when I was younger and I've always been pushed by my mum to have good education. "You never know what you're going to need as a backup plan" I said this to myself to help me mature early on and to balance things, see what's actually important and what I needed to do. Making sure I had a Plan B. My degree and all my other education is completely different to football but without that I might not have been able to keep at it and get up when I get knocked down.

Fortunately, now for women footballers we can earn a comfortable income. I know that maybe 5-10 years ago, that was unheard of but now that the games developed and there is more and more money involved, it is possible to live off earnings as a professional female footballer.

TOP TIPS

1. Listen to your coach or mentor, as generally they do know best. They've got loads of experience. They've

probably lived through a lot of stuff and they're trying to prevent you from going through the same mistakes or path that they went down.

2. Enjoy whatever you're doing. Whether you're a Footballer or a Banker get the best out of yourself and reap the benefits out of what you are doing.

3. Work hard; you get out what you put in. If you really want to get somewhere you have to put in a lot of work. You can't expect stuff to happen by chance.

Future Aspirations

I want to be more involved with England, to get more caps and to score more goals. Club-wise I would like to keep developing and ultimately become a senior player and take on those responsibilities and mature my game in that aspect. Outside of football I'm still in education and doing courses to better myself as once I do finish football I'm going to need something to do at the end of it. So I'm trying to keep myself ticking over and seeing what avenue I want to go down by putting my feet in different waters to see what it is I want to do next.

I WOULD LIKE TO BE REMEMBERED AS...

Ultimately, I would love for people to look up to me once I've finished football and think "I remember when Danielle Carter done this, I would love to do that" For me it's about making memories and having people speak about them in years to come.

DANIELLE CARTER PATHWAY PIT STOP

• Don't be easily led or follow peer pressure
• Prioritise your career; know where you want to end up
• Keep on top of your skills and develop on things you need to improve on
• Be diligent behind closed doors in leading a healthy and nutritious lifestyle.
• Have a Plan B
• Listen to good advice from coach/mentors, enjoy what you're doing and work hard.

DANIELLE CARTER CONTACT DETAILS

Twitter: @DanielleCarter
Instagram: @DanielleCarter

ESRA ÇETIN

Hairstylist

'This trade is amazing, you can go to one of the poorest parts of the world, be in a village and still make money.'

Esra Çetin Prelude
Esra Çetin is the Manager of her own family run business at HWS Salon. She works alongside a talented and professional team offering the latest in hair services ranging from precision cutting to stunning hair colours and beautiful hair-ups for that special occasion or bridal hair. Her client list includes Ruan Du Love, CEO's and top end bankers.

ESRA ÇETIN INTERVIEW

My name is Esra Çetin I am a manager at the HWS Hair Salon in Muswell Hill.

My Love For Hairdressing!

I've always been interested and passionate about Hairdressing. I started off working in a salon at the age of thirteen as a Saturday girl. Being that the salon is a family business and I'm the boss's daughter I experienced loads of obstacles - looking young didn't help as people weren't taking me seriously. They expected me to come in and not do anything so I've always had to work harder than everyone else. Come in an hour earlier, leave an hour later. I've always had to push myself constantly.

I was qualified at the age of seventeen, I worked 7 days a week for 2-3 years doing twelve hour shifts just to get to that point. By the time I hit twenty I was a fully qualified Stylist and Manager.

Hairdressing is difficult because you're always dealing with people one to one. You have to keep your energy levels up and learn and learning how not to take things personally takes a lot of time. Listening to client's problems, what lifestyles they have and how to remember all of that is what keeps you busy in this industry.

Managing a hair salon is hard as I have sixteen people I look after with all their problems and dramas. You have to stay positive because the end game is about making money and that's what you just got to keep thinking about.

Inspirational Parents

My parents were my role models. My dad came here at the age of nineteen with nothing. He left his town in Turkey without any formal education beyond the age of 7 to work in the city as a Hairdresser. He educated himself by learning how to speak English and by the time he hit thirty he had a house and owned the building of our Salon which included the flats upstairs. He's also a silent partner to Landor & Hawa international and I.T Luggage, owns a business in Turkey and has a product distribution company, Keratin Brazilian Blow Dry which gets rid of frizz in the hair. My mum and dad both own the hair salon and perfect shine products. My dad had his fingers in everything, he's such a grafter and so watching him growing up was really inspirational.

My mum on the other hand, she came here (England) when her father died when she was young and so she had to live with my uncles and look after her cousins. She wasn't allowed to educate herself, go swimming or do things like that. She later became a hairdresser and worked together with my dad to build up what they have today. When I was younger, I may not have appreciated them as much but now that I'm older I've realised just how much they did for us. They tried very hard not to bring me and my siblings up with a sliver spoon and made us work for everything.

Point to Prove

When I turned eighteen we had just opened a Salon in St

John's Wood and my Father took me there and he made me the Manager. I couldn't do it, I lasted a year and then ran off. I was very young and naïve.

When I turned twenty-two I had the chance to go back there as a staff member was leaving. Because I had previously ran away, it always ate at me that I didn't achieve what I had set out to do.

When I returned, the Salon was only making £2,500 a week and within 6 months I took it to £7,500 a week. I went in there with only 4 members of staff and by the time it hit a year I had thirteen people working for me.

That was my biggest achievement because I was able to go back and prove myself to the customers. At that particular Salon, a lot of customers weren't nice. They were wealthy, demanding and very patronising. I had customers say things like "You don't know what you're doing, you left school when you were sixteen that's why you're uneducated!"

So, going back was a massive achievement because I learnt how to get people working together as a team and took the Salon from underachieving to being a flourishing business and then able to sell it for a good profit afterwards.

Being Manager and Learning How to Keep a Cool Head

When I was eighteen a customer's wife had a facial done in the salon. The treatment cost £50 and he didn't want to pay the money so he came back and said the beautician scratched her face so that he could get a refund. I asked him if he could bring his wife back to the store so I that I could see her face. He responded by saying "Who do you think you are? Do you know who I am?". That shocked me because at that point I had never experienced anything like that before in my life.

As a manager, you do get your fair share of staff and customer complaints – I've even had staff members start fighting in the middle of the salon and so I've learnt that you have to keep your cool and be level headed especially when you're the manager and that comes with age.

Salons are bitchy, ours isn't thankfully but I try to nip everything in the bud before any tensions arise. Half of people problems are that they don't communicate with each other.

<u>Work Ethic & Routine</u>
I have 2 children so I wake up every day at 5am. I get between 2-3 hours' sleep on average. If I'm working I will stay at my mum's and my husband will look after the children. I get to the shop an hour before work and I'm normally there until 3-4pm treating customers back to back. In 6 hours, I can sometimes do up to ten to thirteen clients and that's on top of the everyday running of the salon taking care of the stock, clients, computers, staff problems and so forth.

I work 5 days a week and I only get one holiday a year.

We run a family business so it comes first as it's our bread and butter, and because we're all in it together it's all of our bread and butter.

Welcome to the Real World

I feel a lot of the younger generation don't listen, they think they know more. Sometimes not saying anything and just listening will get them further. Especially if someone's trying to show you how to do something. Take on board what they're saying, if you don't want to do it - then don't do it. You might not need it today but you might need it in 10 years' time.

Motivate yourself – a lot of young people think work is like school. I tell a lot of my juniors "I'm not your teacher, I'm not going to give you detention or call your mum up and say you haven't worked well. If you haven't worked well, I'll replace you." It's the business world unfortunately.

Continue to educate yourself. Reading is important, you may want to buy a house with your partner one day. You can't rely on them to read the contract. You need to understand how much you need to put in and what the implications are.

Some customers like to talk about politics so keep up-to-date with current events going on around the world. Learn how to put on different faces for different customers.

This Trade is Amazing!
This trade is amazing you can do it from home, you can open up your own place one day, you can even go to one of the poorest parts of the world, be in a village and still make money. Once you become a Stylist it starts from around £21,000 - £30,000 but it does depend on how many customers you bring in and the commission you make. It can even go up higher depending on where you work. If you're freelancing the money is roughly about the same but it's about word of mouth and using social media.

Build Up Your Customer Portfolio
Unfortunately, in this industry people look at you like you're uneducated or a bit of an air head. Because I looked young, initially customers didn't want me to do their hair. I realised I had to bring my knowledge up more, learn to talk better – I was a little bit ghetto back then. I needed that experience because no one teaches you at school that when you work in particular environments you need to talk this way and act this way. So, I changed my hair and the way I dressed because again tracksuits and trainers I felt didn't make me look the part.

In our industry, the way you make money is through customer word of mouth, bookings and having a full column – that's when you make commission and get 40% plus a basic wage. To get that though you need customers to talk about you so you have to sell your persona. It's not about cutting hair; anyone can cut hair, it's about keeping clients. Why should they come back to you? You have to be able to develop a relationship with them.

So, I trained up to get better on my colour knowledge, I read different books and newspapers so that when I managed to get clients such as CEO's and Bankers I had other topics to talk to them about so that they would take me more seriously. When I was working in St Johns Wood I cut hair for high profile clients such as Aisha Caan (Wife of James Caan and their daughters), Ruan Du Love, CEO's and top end bankers. To some people that might sound amazing but to be honest I prefer the family and community clientele we have here in Muswell Hill.

Education
Education from school didn't help me much. Education through life and what my parents taught me, amazing. I'm dyslexic; my secondary school didn't realise until I was fifthteen and so by then I was doing my GCSE's and it was too late. I've always been good with my hands especially in classes like Textiles, Cooking and Technology but when it came to theory I was useless. I couldn't pass anything. So I left school with no GCSE's. Hairdressing was the only thing that clicked.

My dad sent me to a private college which cost £8,000 and he made me sign a contract. It stated that if I messed around like I did in school I would have a year to pay him back. It freaked me out so I really concentrated. I went there Monday-Friday and I worked nights in the Salon as well as weekends. I didn't want to become a hairdresser at twenty-one or twenty-two, I wanted to do it earlier. That's where my dad was really good in the sense that if you didn't do well he would find another way for you to work hard.

TOP TIPS

Find a good salon where you feel you can learn. Don't settle for the first salon you go into. Go for trial dates and explore your options so you can get an idea of the atmosphere at different salons and barbershops. Ask if you will be placed inside a college part time and lastly to stand out from the rest, work harder than the rest and show initiative.

Keep Your Focus
I would say don't allow people to affect you. If someone says you can't do something it doesn't actually mean you can't do it. There are people out there who feed off other people's insecurities and will try and belittle you and make you feel like nothing and you'll find this in every industry and profession. So keep your focus.

At my Salon, I buy all the new staff members the book 'The Secret' and I tell them to set themselves goals and aims every 3 months. It doesn't have to be big just something as little as perfecting how to wash hair or to learn a new treatment or product. After you've achieved that goal set another target.

If you want to become something you have to think about it, dream it, become it and live it to get where you want to go. That would be my biggest advice of all.

I WOULD LIKE TO BE REMEMBERED FOR...

Doing my best, helping others and giving back. I've trained 5 girls that are now working in Central London and elsewhere and I would like for them to feel that I've helped contribute to their success.

ESRA ÇETIN PATHWAY PIT STOP

- Keep your cool and be level headed
- Learn how to get people working together as a team
- Continue to read, motivate and educate yourself
- Listening/taking on board what someone shows you will get you further
- To keep clients, develop a relationship with them. Sell your persona.
- Adapt to your environment, stand out from the rest and show initiative
- Go for trial days at different salons/barbershops.
- Don't allow people to affect you
- If you want to become something you have to think about it, dream it, become it and live it.

ESRA ÇETIN CONTACT DETAILS

Website: www.hwsbeauty.co.uk

ATEF ALSHAER

Lecturer

'I wanted to be a teacher and with this decision it was just a matter of following it through.'

Atef Alshaer Prelude

Atef Alshaer is a Lecturer in Arabic Language and Culture at the university of Westminster. He has published numerous articles and reviews on the culture of the Arab World. He was educated at Birzeit university in Palestine and SOAS, university of London, where he obtained a PhD and taught for a number of years.

ATEF ALSHAER INTERVIEW

My name is Atef Alshaer and I am Lecturer in Arabic
Studies at the university of Westminster. I first came to
the UK in 2003 after completing my Bachelor degree
in English Language and Literature at the university of
Birzeit in Palestine. I then went on to obtain a Masters
and PhD from the faculty of Languages and Cultures at
SOAS, University of London and taught there until 2014.
I have written several research papers and monographs,
including my book, 'Poetry and Politics in the Modern
Arab World' and an edited volume, 'Love and Poetry in
the Middle East'; and 'Language and National Identity in
Palestine: Representations of Power and Resistance in
Gaza'.

My Love for Reading
From an early age, there were teachers that I looked
up to through the eyes of a child. I thought they were
amazing and I wanted to be like them. But as I grew
older and went to university I saw other teachers who
inspired me to be a university lecturer. As I read more
there were other intellectuals that I really admired like
Noam Chomsky and Edward Said. I read a lot of books,
many of those written by authors from my country
and internationally and really all of those people are my
inspirations. I know a lot of incredible people who I've
been inspired by.

Difficulties I Faced Growing Up in Palestine
Palestine is an occupied country, and being under
occupation and living during the Palestine intifada, in

particular between 1987-1993, meant our life was very much surrounded by violence.

Constantly as a child I was faced with pictures of violence that have an impact on you psychologically. That is not how it's supposed to be but then I began to learn about occupation and politics from a very early age.

It taught me that life is not an idyllic thing, it does require learning; learning about yourself, having a profound understanding of what it means to be human in a situation that is entirely inhumane.

I remember times where planes were hovering above in the sky, the sound of bullets all around us, or when some of my relatives or people from our community were getting arrested. I also remember school class mates who were shot and killed or seeing someone return home with their ligaments completely dispatched, riddled by bullets.

This was not only physical violence but also psychological violence because we were exposed to fear on a daily basis. There was a curfew every day from 7 o'clock onwards. You couldn't be out and if you were out, you were afraid. This fear followed not only me throughout my life but Palestinian lives in general.

Violence might surround you or be a constant factor in your life but you carve the spaces out of it for yourself. Within these spaces, you function in a manner that allows you to see a way out of it. Growing up in that environment I personally decided that I wanted to be a teacher and with this decision it was just a matter of following it through.

I was motivated to read more, to reach out more, to talk more, discuss more, to find out more and hopefully in time to engage and help others in similar situations, or not in similar situations; how to stay human in a world which is littered with inhumanity at various levels. Sometimes the dream doesn't seem too immediate enough or you can get distracted by various forces but luck is another factor and we are defined by the opportunities that come our way and I saw mine and I took it.

Love for Languages
I studied English in Gaza from the age of 10. I did my first degree in English at Birzeit university. I have a love for languages in general. I studied English literature and language, history and linguistics. I was a reader from a very young age, I read a lot of stuff in English as well as Arabic and that helped me a great deal but obviously, it's still a language that I'm not innately endowed with. It's not my language (English) but it's a language that I can use fluently. I find it easy to express myself, it's very rich and interesting but Arabic is more the language of my heart.

Happy to be Content
I don't really know if I'm successful but what I do know is that I'm secure. I've written 3 books to date, a novel and sometimes I write poetry. I don't call this success

I call it attempts to reflect what I want to do. Whether these are successes or not, it's not for me to judge. It's for others who use them or don't use them for that matter. I'm quite a content person, I'm happy where I am and I feel fortunate with what I have. Education paved the way for me to be a teacher so in a way I have fulfilled my dream.

My Book 'Poetry and Politics in the modern Arabic world'

The book traces the way in which poets interacted with political events in the Arab world since the nineteenth century. Poetry has always been the most important form of expression in the Arab world since old times and until today to some extent.

These poets talk about the Ottoman Empire, the nation state, the colonial empires and interact with the political events of the day. The colonialism and how Arab poetry responded to colonialism, modern day poetry, the aesthetics of it and how that is expanded politically. How it was enriched or expressed better and all themes that Arab politics has been defined by, whether its secularism, Marxism, Islamists. All these ideologies that have influenced and shaped the Arab world.

I sometimes travel to countries to learn and explore other spaces in the hope of expanding my horizons and indeed my spirit. I also give talks and contribute chapters of my work at conferences.

The Importance of Studying and Revision
To work is a foundation towards success and revision is mastering the thing you want. This should motivate you to achieve the best you can. In academia, sometimes I think that means reading what others have done. Then you can enter a conversation and hold it from its horns in order to understand the process of reasoning; and that doesn't come without work, dedication, time and a sense of independence and commitment.

Salary Expectations
As a lecturer, it depends which university in London but you normally start at £38,000 or so and then progress to earn around £47,000-£58,000 a year, depending on the academic station you have reached. But I think academia is not about money—it is modestly paid; but you could become more spiritually fulfilled than many other fields because you're constantly learning and being challenged. You still have to empathise and sympathise with students from various backgrounds who are there to learn, and I think that's the greatest aspect of academia: learning, empathy and expanding your humanity and hopefully other people's humanity in the process. There is a space and freedom to explore which is quite rare and I think these dimensions can make a better human being out of you. But academia has increasingly become saddled with bureaucratic processes and exchanges which tear away at the spiritually fulfilling and potentially uplifting prospects of learning and understanding.

TOP TIPS

Think of reading and writing as a passion, have a love for understanding the subject you like and use this subject to be creative in your life. Treat yourself and others with mercy, compassion and empathy. There will be difficulties along the way but if you persist and continue you will fulfil your dreams. Look out for opportunities which are related to what you want to do and expand your interests and discover who you are and make efforts to fulfil your potential.

I WOULD LIKE TO BE REMEMBERED AS...

A good person to family, friends, students and whoever I came across; all else is less significant.

ATEF ALSHAER PATHWAY PIT STOP

• We are defined by opportunities that come our way
• Mastering the work you do is the foundation towards success
• Think of reading and writing as a passion and have love for the subject you are learning

ATEF ALSHAER CONTACT DETAILS

Website: Link to book
www.hurstpublishers.com/book/poetry-and-politics-in-the-modern-arab-world/

AKALA

Music Artist

'It's important to think about the things we place value on.'

Akala Prelude

Akala is a BAFTA and MOBO award-winning hip-hop artist, writer and social entrepreneur, as well as the co-founder of the Hip-Hop Shakespeare Company. He has written for and appeared on the BBC, Channel 4 News, Question Time, The Guardian, the Huffington Post and the Independent. His online lectures and performances, including Oxford Union and TEDx, have millions of views on YouTube.

AKALA INTERVIEW

My name is Akala I am a Hip Hop Artist, Writer and
Social Entrepreneur. I founded a small record label called
Illa State Records and an education and music theatre
company called the The HipHop Shakespeare Company.

Investment

One of the ways I started was very early in 2004 when I
got some investment. I teamed up with a producer and we
started a label together. The challenges were trying to be
a politically conscious hip hop artist. I realised very early
that I was never going to get on the radio and therefore I
had to develop a whole new business model based around
being independent. But I am lucky to exist in a time where
the internet exists. It's meant that for people who want
an alternative point of view there is a way of getting that
across more easily than at any other point in time in
history.

My Influences

My role models growing up, beside from family, were
people like Chuck D from Public Enemy, Jimmy Hendricks,
Bob Marley, and Dennis Brown – they were my musical
influences. I loved Football so I loved people like Ian
Wright and Dennis Bergkamp as I played football for a
long time.

Making a Positive Impact

My biggest success is the impact I'd like to think some
of the stuff I've made has had on other people's thinking.
I'm not presuming that; it's what people tell me every

day. When mothers have messaged me, and said their sons stayed in school as they're inspired by the message I spread and unlike most kind of Hip-Hop it encourages them to be smart and take pride in their intelligence. So when I see in real ways some of the stuff I've tried to create has affected other people for the better that makes me really proud.

Responding to Challenges

The whole time I grew up we didn't have money. My mum's white, my dad's black. I grew up in London. There were loads of reasons. My mum got very sick when I was young and her and my step dad split up. I went through my little phase of thinking I'm a 'rude boy' and misbehaving.

My life is always about challenges and I think that if you can respond to those challenges and disappointments in a positive and open minded way - even if angry, you can channel that anger constructively and use that adversity, then it can be of benefit sometimes.

Work Ethic & Routines

I must admit I am disciplined to the point that it annoys me! For instance, at the beginning of every year I'll write up in my note book this is how many training sessions I want to do. This is how much books I want to complete. Where most people feel like "yeah I am going to read a book" I'll schedule that into my diary. So, say from 9-11am will be my reading time. 11-1pm will be training time and so on. I don't always stick to it but I'll stick to it most of the time and it's the way I get most things done by managing my time.

I have a team which includes 2 managers, the staff at The HipHop Shakespeare Theatre and a network of people around me that partner with me to help make things run efficient as possible. I don't have one routine as I fly all over the world and do many things, as does my company. So, I have many routines contradicting with one another at once. Time is the most valuable resource we have. So I try managing my time as strictly as possible.

Balancing It All Out

I don't think I do find that balance of quality time with friends and family amongst my personal commitments. I think that naturally if you live what you do and you're an artist and you're lucky enough to make a living from your art, it can dominate your life and it can mean you don't make as much time as you probably should for the people that you love.

Pitfalls to Avoid

For me it depends on what the kind of artist the young person wants to be. If you want to be a here today gone tomorrow type of 'pop artist' I can't advise you on that. If you want to have longevity and an actual career as an artist then the pitfall I would avoid is buying into hype, buying into style over substance - where buying into the appearance of success is more important than actual success. Those things are the very serious pitfalls for people to be aware of when getting into the music industry.

What It Takes To Be An MC

If you're an MC you need the skills of an MC. Flow, delivery, decent enough sounding voice, ability to perform well and being a good songwriter. Being a good rapper and being a good songwriter are two very different things. Then in terms of the business side of things you've got to be reliable.

If you're going to be an independent artist like me, your word has to mean something. People have got to be able to trust you're going to turn up. You've got to be disciplined and take on multiple skills sets. You've got to be good at managing other people.

People management is the number one skill that a business owner needs. From my perception and I won't lie or be overly humble, it's clear I have a certain amount of influence just like Chuck D or on a bigger level the Wu Tang Clan had on me and I am very well known to a certain audience - young multi-ethnic inner city working class Britain.

Understanding Residual Income

In the music industry, there are people that are billionaire's, there are people in the music industry that are making no money at all – they're losing money. For me and the journey that I've been on it's about ownership of your own future and building a legacy. There's one thing of earning money - we all want to earn money and I make a very decent living. I'm not going to pretend I don't, I do, but I also own the two companies that put out all my material and I'm about to set up a third business. The difference is there's a legacy, it's what you call 'residual income', a means of making money while you're asleep not doing anything. Whether it's from royalties, book sales, or internet views etc. We live in a world where it's easier than at any time before to make money off of something you only had to do once. So it's about young people understanding residual income as well.

Education Isn't Just About What Happens In School

My level of education has been invaluable to me. Education isn't just about what happens in school. I barely went to college and I didn't go to university but I run businesses and most people who went to university don't run businesses. I've been self-educated, I've studied myself, I've travelled, I've thought about the way the world is and where I want to be in that scheme of things as an Artist and I've tried to shape what I do on those assumptions. This came from how I grew up, influences, luck and personal choice. I don't believe you just choose, I think your choices are made in context with other factors in your life. Yes, I made some positives choices but I've made some bad choices that I wasn't punished for. When I was sixteen/seventeen and a bit of a naughty boy I never ended up in jail so I think all of these things connect in an interesting way.

TOP TIPS

Discipline, dedication and value. Discipline and dedication are probably obvious but I think it's important to think about the things we place value on. It's important to make money and I'll repeat I make a very good living, I have a very nice car and I live in one of the most expensive parts of London, life is good. I'm not knocking anyone for making their money but what I am saying is that the things that we place value on are important. There should be things we're not willing to do for money. I could have made loads more money if I was willing to do things that are against my principles. I get offered every week to do things that are against my principles for lots of money and if I don't like the idea, because my integrity is more valuable to me than money, I say no!

Create art that makes value not just money. Value that uplifts people and value that inspires people. I think values are really, really important.

Inspirations

What inspires me are people who have risked their lives often or their livelihoods to make a world a better place. The Muhammad Ali's, the Bob Marley's, Malcolm X's. The people that have said "I can't live in the world as it is." So my music is also political and tries to inspire people and imagine a better and different future. Showing young people there's another way to be successful and keeping your integrity.

In 2014 I published a graphic novel called the Ruins of Empire which did really well and I've finished writing a comic with Juan Carlos Baez from Puerto Rico and a new music EP. Writing and publishing is where I am looking to have a real impact going forward.

Writing Lyrics Without Using Pen and Paper

When I was younger I heard Jay-Z say how he would write songs in his head without using a pen and paper and I thought "Nah, that's impossible!" So, I started looking in my own note books and noticed that I was only noting the end words of the sentences already, so that would trigger the whole sentence. So, then I stopped writing stuff down.

Sometimes if I'm making an album and I've got loads of songs to do quickly then I will write it down but none of my "Fire in the booth" (BBC 1Xtra Charlie Sloth Rap Show Freestyle Segment) for example were ever written on paper. I just listen to the beat, write the lyrics in my head and eventually I memorised the entire thing and went ahead and rapped it on the show. I wouldn't say the process is quicker but it can be a lot more fun and you organise stuff in your head rather than writing it down and committing to one way of doing it. It becomes like a jig-saw puzzle that fits together.

10 Year Album Anniversary

I'm proud that it's been 10 years since my first album and to have done my biggest UK tour and touring around the world. Over that span of time I've really learnt and feel vindicated having proven that the long run, the hard slog and having the integrity and the willingness to not sell out pays off.

I WOULD LIKE TO BE REMEMBERED AS...

Someone that inspired people to seek knowledge.

AKALA PATHWAY PIT STOP

• Learning to channel anger and disappointment in a constructive way can sometimes be of benefit
• Manage your time effectively
• To be an MC you need the skills of an MC
• Being a rapper and a songwriter are two completely different things
• People management is the number one thing a business owner needs
• Understand the mechanics of residual income
• Education isn't just about what happens in school
• The things we place value on are important
• Create art that makes value not just money

AKALA CONTACT DETAILS

Twitter: @Akalamusic
Instagram: @Akalamusic
Website: www.akalmusic.com
Website: www.hihopshakespeare.com

CHAKA CLARKE

Personal Trainer

'The best competition is where everybody wins'.

Chaka Clarke Prelude
Chakabars Clarke is a Personal Trainer/community athlete and social entrepreneur based in London. He played an instrumental role as part of the Love Army for Somalia social media GoFundMe campaign which went viral in March 2017, to support the famine relief and help raise close to £2m in aid and arrange for Turkish Airlines to donate a plane to carry food and provisions to the country.

CHAKA CLARKE INTERVIEW

My name is Chaka Clarke I am a Personal Trainer, I run a fitness movement organisation called SpartanFam. I'm also a Social Entrepreneur.

How I started out as a Personal Trainer

I started after I left the army. I was training troops in the army to get them fit for deployment in Iraq and Afghanistan but then doing more reading and learning I decided that I definitely didn't agree with the British Governments Foreign Policy. When I left I not only realised that I was very fit but that I'm also a good people's person and I could help to educate people physically about themselves and make them interested in their health and fitness. So, I did a personal training course when I left the army and I've been training people ever since then.

Family Members Shaped Me

I was really into athletics and when my cousin, Marlon Devonish was going through the peaks of his career he really inspired me. I remember my dad trained him when he was younger and he is one of the only British Caribbean men representing Britain to ever win a gold medal when he captained the 4x100 metres team at the Athens Olympics in 2004. But I think the only person I had growing up was my mum. Things happen in life and I haven't seen my dad in nearly twenty years and so my mum raised me, my brother and my sister, she was our world. Just the way she was able to keep us fed, keep us healthy, we were never sick when we were growing up because we were vegan and she just kept us going. It was that discipline she had that inspired me and my siblings.

Staying True to Myself
I'd say probably one of my biggest adversities was trying to remain true to myself, my morals, my values and my culture at the same time as trying to be a successful commercial trainer. It was very difficult thing to do as at one point in time as I was sponsored by a particular company but because of the way that company appropriates black culture to make a lot of money for its shareholders and owners, plus the fact that we didn't have much creative control, I became fed up with them and said "I'm done!" as I really didn't want to work with them anymore. I also speak out politically, about knowledge of self, racism, sexism and all the things that I think are important given our current social, economic and political situation.

Day in A Life
I will get up in the morning I will have some loose leaf organic tea, then I'll have water and fruits - my main breakfast meal which will be steamed hard food and green veg - yam, green banana, plantain, and sweet potato. Then I'll go out and start training my clients depending on how many I've got on that day. If I have 3 clients in the day time then I'll try and have a lunch after that. Then I'll have maybe 2 more clients and various meetings in the afternoon, then more clients or classes in the evening whilst fitting in my own training once a day. So, it's quite work based, I don't really have that

much time off but because I'm self-employed I make it that way.

SpartanFam Company

My friend Charlie Dark, runs a crew called 'Run Dem Crew' he said to me "The last time I saw you, you were about to get on a train and go to Iraq. Now you're down here and you've got this amazing story"

When I was down in Leeds training with my friend in a park some guys came and shot him in the face with a shotgun and murdered him. A month after his death I became depressed. He was a boxer and a trainer too – it had nothing to do with drugs or money or anything like that, just an altercation that went too far. Nobody deserves murder he didn't even deserve a slap. In that moment, I asked myself if I was to die tomorrow would I be proud of my life and proud of my achievements and the answer was no.

But prior to all this happening, I had already decided I was going to move to London and train celebrities, drive a Range Rover or Aston Martin and then when that incident happened I thought what will I have to show for my life if that's all I do?

So, I started reading some books, I had just moved to London as I had to appear in the murder trial. During that time, I had a meeting with Charlie and he said "What you're doing is amazing. You should tell people, show people, start training people." I've often found that training inside gyms are just a terrible experience. So, I said let's train outdoors and make it about socialising. I ran a free fitness class for a year and a half and that's how Spartan Family came about. I decided to run a fitness class so anybody and everybody could come down and we focus it around the slowest and the weakest. We used social media to help it grow. Loads of 'known' people endorsed it. We grew it from there and now we run 4 fitness classes a week and we're expanding those classes. It's organic and nobody owns it except me and the people. It's not something that can be bought out because it's for the community essentially.

Maintaining a healthy and balanced lifestyle with friends and family

I don't do this as well as I would like to. I speak a lot with my mum and sister on the phone, they still live in Leeds and I live in London. What I try to do with my friends is arrange things for us to do. I'm one of those people that if I'm in a space and I'm evolving, growing, changing and shaping positively I try and bring people with me. So rather than me go and eat at the same place we used to go eat at I'd bring them to the new places I'm going to eat at. Or rather than me go to the club I'll say "I'm not going to go the club but there's this training session tomorrow, if you want to come we can meet there and socialise, chat rubbish or whatever." Ultimately, I'm trying to create my own community wherever I go with people who not only love themselves but love each other.

Pitfalls to Avoid

Try not to be used too much. What can happen is you can be magnificently strong or very attractive or have great ideas and the people who are essentially running fitness are very quick to use somebody to make them more money without ever giving back.

They'll be a million Personal Trainers and only a few of them will stand out and be around for the next twenty years, the reason being you end up not being owned.

So, for instance you sign a contract with a gym like I did when I first moved down to London whereby I was working at a fitness gym and paying them £800 a month rent and was only earning £1,000 a month. Their profit was big just from me to be able to use their facilities but I was really struggling. These people don't care about how brilliant you are, so like anything in life start your own organic business, and essentially start something that you have creative control over.

In school, they teach you to work 9-5, almost a factory farm job to make somebody else rich and make somebody else money. But the people who run the world are taught to create businesses. To create a business is something your kids can inherit, it means you can take your own time off work when you see fit, you can do things essentially that somebody who works a 9-5 in an office or for Tesco is never going to be able to do. Everybody's had a job they hate and everybody's had the career that they might get lost in. However, a business that you have control of and is ultimately going to pay your pension is something where you'll go to work happy as your giving back to yourself and not to somebody else.

<u>Team Work Makes the Dream Work!</u>
Initially when I first started out I thought everybody was my rival. They're not as good as me, there not as fit as me, they're not as strong as me, they don't know as much as me. Then I realised that we're all human beings and that all of those people are my brothers and my sisters and the way that I managed to be successful was by including everybody. Meeting and reasoning with all the other trainers, nutritionists, massage therapists and building up a network of people that when I needed them for an event or to share ideas I could call on them. That made me far more successful. The best competition is where everybody wins.

<u>Being an Influencer Generates Income</u>
In London, the starting price per hour to hire a Personal Trainer is £50. The reason why it's so high is because they need a certain number of clients to be able to earn a certain amount to live on. Music artists regularly pay their trainer to go on tour with them and they can earn £300 a day, get all of their expenses paid and come home with £6,000 - £7,000 grand in their pocket within the space of two weeks whereby that could have usually taken them 4 months. It depends where you want to be. If you work really hard and have a plan you can do whatever, but if nobody notices you then nobody's going to refer you, book you or be interested in you.

A really good tool to use is social media. So, speaking with various different people on social media, learning the latest social media platforms and how it works and becoming an influencer. Once you become an influencer then you can not only influence other people you can influence your own financial income.

I've trained various people from different backgrounds including singers, songwriters, models, actors - a lot of people in the entertainment industry as their physical appearance is important in their field of work. I was training Emily Goulding for a while, Chase and Status; really affluent business people like the heads of big banks, that sort of thing. But for me the best people that I train are pupils in schools and young people in prisons (Young Offender's Institutes) where I run educational and community led programmes.

Education

My level of academic education has contributed a very minimal role. My knowledge of self and self-education has contributed massively. In my opinion, academia has been created to stop people thinking, teaching people what to think not how to think. It's all well and good teaching people what to think in order to do a certain job role but if you can teach people how to think in order to create wealth and business then it doesn't really matter. Most of the richest people in the world didn't go to university.

Top Tips

You need to be disciplined, have a drive and a motivation

to keep yourself fit and healthy and find happiness in what you're doing. Whatever product you are trying to sell you should embody it and live it. It should be a lifestyle. It takes a lot of dedication. There's going to be times when you're broke and annoyed at life but you have to persevere. For two years, I was broke and now I earn a very healthy amount of money, take holidays when I want and I have true power because it's created by me.

What is the Purpose?

Probably the biggest question is "What is the purpose?" And that can manifest itself in many different ways but this is a question that anybody who is starting any sort of career or living any sort of life or has any thoughts on their mind needs to define early on. It will change, it's transient but if you don't ever ask yourself that then you will be lost for a long time. If you don't know where you're going, then any pathway will lead you there. So, you need to ask yourselves very early on "What is my purpose? What is my reason for being?" Once you get that everything else will be easy. I found mine a long time ago and that's why I can continually work in the same energy and be able to be positive every day.

I WOULD LIKE TO BE REMEMBERED AS...

I would like to finish by saying "Without a revolution of health there's not a revolution of consciousness. If people have a vessel that's polluted, then they can never have a thought set free. I'd like to be remembered as somebody who affected the lives of people positively nothing more, nothing less.

CHAKA CLARKE PATHWAY PIT STOP

- Remain true to yourself, your morals and values
- Try not to be used
- Having a business that you control is something that your kids can inherit and can pay your pension
- Be disciplined – have a drive and motivation to keep yourself fit and eat healthy food
- Whatever product you are trying to sell you should embody it and live the lifestyle
- Learn how to use social media platforms to speak to people and become an influencer
- Ask yourself what is the purpose?

CHAKA CLARKE CONTACT DETAILS

Twitter: @Chakabars
Instagram: @Chakabars
Website: www.spartanfam.com

MICHAEL WHARLEY

Photographer

'Follow your sense of creativity and skill.'

<u>Michael Wharley Prelude</u>
Michael Wharley is a BIPP (British Institute of
Professional Photography) award winning professional
Photographer whose work can be seen over in spotlight,
as well as in national newspapers & magazines, on film
posters across the London Underground and at venues
like the National Theatre.

MICHAEL WHARLEY INTERVIEW

My name is Michael Wharley I'm a photographer specialising in the entertainment industry. I take portraits for actors and take the images that you might see on a film or theatre poster.

Finding My Way

I went to university, then drama School for a year and worked as an actor for 6 years. I had a lovely time doing that and then towards the end of being an actor, although I was quite fortunate with work, something wasn't very satisfying in my life. I gradually worked out that unfortunately it was being an actor. At the time, I was doing a show and decided that when it finished so should I; that it was time to do something else.

I was interested in photography, but the immediate obstacle I faced was confidence - not knowing whether I was good enough to reach the standard to be a professional. Money was a problem too; photography's a very expensive profession and anyone thinking about that career is going to have to invest some money, time and effort into getting it going and getting the equipment they need.

Following My Intuition

My biggest success was following my intuition; that's the thing I'm most proud of in my life. Following what felt right. In terms of the single biggest achievement as an individual, that would be getting my business going from scratch and going from someone who was not very skilful with a camera, to being someone quite skilled with a camera, as well as running a business with a recognised 'brand' and being known within the industry as an expert.

For any pathway into a creative profession it's a balance between your instincts, talents and sensibility. I went on a brilliant course in Brixton at PhotoFusion where I learnt about film and dark room photography. I was interested in portraiture so I tried to turn every bit of the course to learning about taking portraits of people. Teaching can only take you so far though; you've got to work out your approach for yourself and the only way to do that is - in the case of photography - taking photo after photo after photo.

When I reach a point when something feels lacking technically, I find a course where someone can teach me the technique. There's so much information on YouTube and online resources. There's almost nothing that you can't find a video for where someone tells you how to do it and that's such an incredible resource. I would advise anyone thinking about a creative profession to use that.

When The Going Gets Tough

Starting the business, particularly in my late twenties, was very difficult. I didn't always have enough money to go out with friends, buy new clothes, go to the cinema and was eating a lot of baked potatoes! It definitely had an effect on my quality of life, but I knew that when I started the business that it was going to involve that. Fortunately, I've come out the other side and have a better work-life balance. I think you get through the set-up phase by being clear about what you want to achieve, and what you're willing to sacrifice; that gives you a structure to hang on to when times are a little bit tough.

Having A Timetable Helps!

The job is all day every day, if I'm not shooting for a client, I'm planning the next shoot, or I'm doing my own creative work, going over the accounts, making a new website or rebranding. One of the joys of a photographic career is that you are what you do and there's something really satisfying about that. It gives you a lot of heart and a lot of wholeness when you go home at the end of the day.

It does pay to think carefully about investing in yourself as well as the business, because work can become a bit of a drug. Putting time, money and effort into the business makes the business better. But if you're not careful you can end up investing only in your business and not yourself.

In terms of scheduling, I shoot a certain number of portrait sessions a week. I've built a timetable that allows me to make money but be creative. Earlier in my career there's no question it was a bit harder to book a holiday or have the confidence to know my clients weren't going to abandon me. You really do have to work extremely hard when you're starting out.

Balancing It All Out

If you're someone who values a really rigid structure to your time, it's possible that a career like photography isn't for you. You might want a 9-5 job where you're working with a community of people all the time and have really set goals. You can go home at the end of the day play

5-a-side (football) with your mates and go to the pub on the weekend. Then start again on Monday. There's nothing wrong with that.

Many things sustain us; family, friends, hobbies, and the creative satisfaction you get from the job and running a business well. If you're running your own creative business, you get a lot of fulfilment from work, but I've learned the hard way that it's important to make sure you set aside time for family and friends, and to do the things that sustain you outside work.

Pitfalls to Avoid

Avoid envy! It's very easy to only see the success in someone else's career, but what you're seeing is the result of 5, 10, 15 years of hard work. So, don't look at other people and judge yourself against them. Like their work, aspire to do work as good as them, pick apart their work to understand how they have succeeded, and use that to help you. Trust that your artistic sensibility; what you bring to a photo, a job, a client relationship is unique.

People Hire Photographers for Their Unique Take on The World

To be successful you need to be very hard working, and have exceptional client skills. I don't think the old idea of the 'diva' photographer is valid any more. You've got to be easy to get on with, really efficient and good at your job: those things will make people want to hire you.

People also hire photographers for their unique take on the world. So, make sure you really try and differentiate yourself from the competition. If you're an artist be clear about who you are so that people understand what they're getting from you.

I have always tried to make my website and information available about me online very transparent. When I started out I looked at the competition and I thought there was a space in the market for someone who identified themselves very clearly as an expert. So, I had some very good branding done and I made sure everywhere I advertised or appeared my branding was the same. And I set myself up as an expert, someone who knew about headshots, as well as taking them, someone who was an authority in the industry.

Perhaps I hadn't earned the right to do that at that point in my career! But I do believe that you should pitch yourself as being where you actually want to be in 3-4 years. It helps other people understand you and your work. Fortunately, through hard work and a bit of luck I'm now known in the industry as being a good photographer, but also as a headshot expert; so, the fronting paid off!

Money, money, money

With photography, the sky's the limit in terms of income, but the average wage is probably low. The industry really values young, fresh ideas. There are Instagrammers who've become fashion photographers. People who are fourteen years old being discovered and shooting for magazines like Vogue, or people who work for fifthteen years without hitting it big. There isn't a guaranteed fast track, but hard work and discipline will pay off.

In commercial photography, I know of photographers who do 10 shoots a year and earn perhaps up to £100,000 for a shoot. That's the very, very top end. You could work as a wedding photographer and you might be able to charge £1,000 - £5,000 for a wedding and could do as many as £15,000 - £40,000 a year. With family and baby portraiture it would be somewhere between £50 - £200 a session, and you'd be shooting a lot. It's reasonable to expect somewhere up to a six-figure turnover if you run your business well.

But the thing with photography is you have very high fixed costs. Your equipment's expensive, your studio rent is expensive and you use a lot of electricity. The costs of running the business will always be quite high. However, if you can sell yourself right; people will pay good money for good photos.

Education
I don't think you need a university or Master's Degree to be good at taking images. It's a visual skill, it's an aesthetic and it's a sense of creativity. There's nothing that is technically difficult about cameras and lighting. The first time you go into a studio you think "How the hell do I use these lights?!" Use them for two years and it's almost second nature, they are simply tools to express yourself, rather than complex machines.

I've had a good education; I went to Oxford for university and Central School for Speech and Drama for an MA and those things have both been really useful in the running of the business and definitely helped me get a bit further, but it didn't make me take better photos.

Other people will go to somewhere like London College of Communications or Central St Martins and they'll do a photography qualification. What it will give you is a history of photography, contemporary photography and your place in the spectrum of photographic possibility. All of those things you can learn from going to exhibitions, reading books and being online. I don't think anyone thinking about a career in photography should think there's any route they have to follow. Follow your sense of creativity and skill.

TOP TIPS

Work incredibly hard, be incredibly nice and have faith in your skills and your artistry.

If I could give myself a bit of advice about starting up now I'd say "Trust you're not on the outside, everyone else isn't great and you're bad. Trust that the way you see things is interesting" and if you carry on working at it, you'll take photos that people will want to look at, or pay you to take.

I WOULD LIKE TO BE REMEMBERED AS...

Someone creative, successful in business and as an artist, and who always made his clients feel they were the most important thing in the world.

MICHAEL WHARLEY'S PATHWAY PIT STOP

• Follow your intuition
• Find courses to do that can add to your skillset and use online videos to learn new techniques
• Don't look at other people and judge yourself against them
• If you enjoy a rigid structure and lifestyle a creative career may not be for you
• Set aside time for family, friends and take part in things that sustain you outside work
• Be hard working, have good interpersonal skills and try to manage your subjects well
• There isn't a guaranteed fast track – hard work and discipline will get you pay off
• Have faith in your skills and your artistry.

MICHAEL WHARLEY'S CONTACT DETAILS

Twitter: @MichaelWharley
Instagram: @MichaelWharley
Website: www.michaelwharley.com
Website: www.michaelwharleyphoto.com
Facebook: /michaelwharleyphotography

AARON DOUGLAS-LETTS

Plumber

'Never give up at the first hurdle. Get used to hearing no's but expect a yes.'

Aaron Douglas-Letts Prelude

Aaron Douglas-Letts is a dynamic man who at a young age became a London City based entrepreneur and business owner. He has been a business owner for over thirteen years and is an active inspirational public speaker, people motivator, international philanthropist and humanitarian.

AARON DOUGLAS-LETTS INTERVIEW

My name is Aaron Douglas-Letts I'm a plumber, gas engineer and small business owner based in London.

Super Mum!

My best role model to date is my mum. She inspires me as she is very hard working. When I was young she was the driving force to my success even down to me getting a paper round job. She was the type of woman to say when you get up in the morning keep pushing, she gave me the freedom to express myself, she was my role model and idol. My mum would say "If you've got a job and still don't have enough money, get another job. That was my mum's method. She used to work on Christmas day, New Year's Day, there were no days off for my mum even if she was sick she'd work and that's where she sowed that seed of the importance of working in me from a young age.

Choosing The Right Career

My biggest success to date was choosing the right career. This career has provided so many things for myself, my family and I've been able to inspire so many people. They say wisdom is known by its children, meaning if you've got wisdom it will show. I didn't originally want to do plumbing I wanted to be a mechanic because I used to get my hands dirty and fix bikes.

When I was younger, me and my twin brother (Byron) had a drying room outside of our flat that was used for storage. We used to turn it into a bike shed and fix bikes for free. Everyone would come. I wouldn't charge anyone; I didn't have business skills back then but I had a trade and that's where it started; me just being able to take things a part and fix it and so mechanics was the next step.

But when I went to see my Grandad (who's passed away) he said to me "I don't think you should do mechanics" and I said "Why?" He said "Because it's a greasy job you come home and your dirty, it's greasy." So, I said "What I am going to do then? He rocked back on his chair and he crossed his legs and he looked at the boiler and said "That!" and he pointed to the boiler. I said "What's that?' I didn't even know what it was at the time. He said "You want to know how to fix them. If you know how to fix them, you'll go clear" and that was my eureka moment. My grandad was originally the person who said I should be a boiler engineer.

Believing in Myself

I recognised that the greatest adversary for people these days are not situations or people but themselves. My greatest adversary is myself. I didn't start looking at people and get inspired, I got competitive, but you've got to stick in your own grace or you end in disgrace. My grace was fixing things so I knew what I was good at. As I laboured in what I did, I got better at it and gained more belief. The greatest problem that I had was believing in myself. "I can achieve it if I just believe".

There are no two people with the same finger print.

I am my own person so when I realised that I didn't watch anybody else or envy them. Look at your own situations and say "You know what I'm going to work on myself."

Work Ethic & Routines

Routine's very important, I'm a man of faith so I pray in the morning spiritually to edify my spirit. Having a balanced diet in terms of success is one of the main goals. If you have a car you keep your car serviced, in my field of work you've got to make sure your body is right as it's labour intensive. So make sure you're in shape and have the right nutrients in you. What's the point in having money if you can't move?

I started out as a sole trader and now I've converted it into a company base structure. In the beginning, I had to do everything myself. I didn't take into consideration family time or me time. It was all work, work, work. When you're zealous and you're young you want to do as much work as you can in the quickest time possible but now I have administrators. So, the work comes in, we assign it to the administrators and they structure it out accordingly as to who is available.

Behind Every Good Man There's a Great Woman

My wife is the heart of my success. We were a young couple but you grow, you mature and you learn to work together as a team and my wife is the backbone of my structure. Without her I can't stand. She would encourage me and look after our children while I'm at work. Behind every good man there's a great woman. She makes everything work, without her it would not work this way. Looking back now I can see how vital she was to the formula of success. I can't go out there and do many jobs for customers if my house is not in check, it's a problem. This is where compromising with the wife comes from, so now I structure it with work, family life, church and friends. I run a tight ship in my household as it's very, very busy. We have 4 kids and it's very hard to balance it all. The key to it is one day at a time will get you through.

Pit falls to Avoid

I've had a lot of apprentices over the years. It's hard to get them up and going as there's a lot of deception and false images of how young men should be. Growing up I was trying to get young people to take on my trade but the problem I had is that they wanted quick money. So what I would say to young people now is it's not about quick money it's about consistency, patience and being realistic with yourself.

It's like a seed, look at a tree for example, a tree doesn't start out as a tree, it's a seed. If you water the seed, it grows. If someone says they can "make you a million pounds tomorrow", they're lying to you. The way a business man has success and makes millions is by doing small things well. So, as you do small things well you'll do big things well.

A lot of young people that got trained with me in college were looking at the TV, the hip hop lifestyle, and saying they want to make that type of money. Even the rappers and the music artists weren't making that kind of money. But it's what you don't see that these young people have to be careful about. The ground work, the motive and the drive. If you make quick money, it's going to go quick. "Easy come easy go." Whereas if you take your time it's not easy for that money to go.

Keep Consistent

Being humble is a big, big thing. The culture that I come from, you're pride full, you take what you want; if you want it you take it. To get in this trade you have to humble yourself and you keep knocking on that door, the door will open.

I found getting into this trade very difficult. Out of every hundred people I rang only one would say come down for an interview. So, I started thinking I've got to call around four to five hundred people to get at least 5 yeses. So I grabbed the yellow pages and I kept consistent.

Humility; to do what you normally wouldn't do to get your foot in the door. Some people give up at the first hurdle, that's the mistake; never give up at the first hurdle. Get used to hearing no's but expect a yes.

Climbing The Ladder

The steps of plumbing are you start out as a young apprentice earning around £40 - £50 a day cash in hand. Plus you have to go college to get qualifications. After 5 years you can get a job working for someone else as an employee and look towards earning £35,000 starting wage but that's with the qualifications of having your gas certificate. If you choose to do your own thing i.e. start your own company and get your advertising right the sky is absolutely the limit. You can't put a price on how much you can earn because everyone has got a need for hot water and heating and if the boilers not broken then it's the tap or the drain etc.

It's a massive industry. You've got to decide what you want to do. You can't do everything but you can own a company that can do everything.

The first year I came straight out of college and started my company I made about £70,000 turnover. Profit margin around £30 - £40k so not only did I make what I would have made working for someone else, but I made quite a substantial amount of income for myself and that was in 2006. Things have gone up! It's extraordinary how much money you can earn. It's a very, very good trade.

Education
I wasn't keen on education and my mum wasn't keen on education either. The way I was raised was you go out there and work and I thought there was a problem in that.

It's good to work but you have to work smarter. At one point, I had 3 jobs and I still didn't have enough money in my pocket and other people had one job and that was enough.

When I recognised this error, I thought there must be

something else I can do. So, I decided that in order for me to get where I wanted to go I needed qualifications. But qualifications nowadays in 2018 are not necessary in this trade. If I had to pick between a guy with experience and a guy with qualifications I would take the guy with experience. Why? Because the worlds moving faster, and as the world moves faster you need people with experience. People with qualifications haven't got experience. The people with experience haven't got qualifications but once you get the experience you can go back to college to get the qualifications you need. It's much harder getting the experience out in the field.

If you're from a broken home background where nobody has been to university or college, don't be discouraged. It's all about how hard you are willing to work as you can always go back and retake your tests.

I was a college dropout. I went college for 2 years and because they were holding me back I dropped out. I had a choice, learn more experience or stay in college and be slow. I was ahead of the other students. They were cutting copper piping and I was fitting in boilers. I was thinking I can't stay here I've got to go out there in the field and then go back to college later. So, I dropped out to get experience and then went back to college a few years later to get my ACS (Gas Qualification Certificate.)

TOP TIPS

Don't take no for an answer and don't see yourself bigger than you are. Stay in your lane like a car or an athlete and focus on what you're doing.

Learn to follow; everyone with authority is under authority. Learn to come under someone because if you can't learn how to come under someone then you can't be over no one. Every leader has been a follower at some time so learn how to follow and submit under someone else.

I WOULD LIKE TO BE REMEMBERED AS...

I want to be remembered for helping people, especially my family. Family comes first. I would like people to say that guy helped me, that guy talked to me, that guy inspired me, that guy loved. The Bible says 'It's more a blessing to give than to receive'. I don't want to be the richest man in the grave yard. It's not about money but in this life, it can help. I would like to be remembered as a guy who gave his all, loved and never gave up.

AARON DOUGLAS-LETTS PATHWAY PIT STOP

- Stick in your grace or you'll end in disgrace
- The greatest adversary for people these days are themselves
- One day at a time will get you through
- It's not about quick money it's about consistency,

patience and being realistic with yourself
• If you do small things well, you'll do big things well
• Humble yourself and have humility to get your foot in the door
• Never give up at the first hurdle – get used to hearing no's but expect a yes
• Work hard but work smarter
• Learn how to come under somebody

AARON DOUGLAS-LETTS CONTACT DETAILS

Website: www.cityboilerrepair.co.uk
Email: info@cityboilerrepair.co.uk

RIA HEBDEN

Presenter

'Anything's possible if you put your mind to it'

Ria Hebden Prelude
Ria Hebden is a Presenter with an impressive portfolio of work. She was selected as the official red-carpet presenter at the MOBO awards in Leeds 2015 and regularly hosts prestigious industry awards shows and panel discussions for the Royal Television Society's Futures Committee, the Media Production Show and the TriForce Short Film Festival.

RIA HEBDEN INTERVIEW

My name is Ria Hebden. I am a Presenter/Broadcaster and I would like to think I'm also a motivational inspirer.

Getting My Foot in The Door

I started out working in television after I had completed a joint degree in Film and Television with American Studies at Brunel university. I was quite lucky as I had a friend who worked at TalkBack Thames at the time who gave me a heads up that they were looking for runners and I was asked to attend an interview and got offered the job.

That for me, was the perfect place to start my career in media because at that time Talkback (now owned by Fremantle Media) was on Newman Street in Soho and under one roof worked the production teams, writers, the talent management team, editors and the publicity team. So, I had an amazing glimpse of how to write a TV programme, how to film it, how you put it together and then how you package it together and publicise it. That was a real blessing to have had that opportunity and to have worked with some amazingly talented people at the same time.

Having worked as a runner for a year my media career grew, I went on to work on productions such as 'X Factor' season two, a documentary called 'Indian Finishing School' at Diverse Productions and on 'Big Brother' season four which was one of the best jobs in the world. I love the thrill of live telly and I was on location in Elstree surrounded by really creative people. Everything was happening at an exciting pace and I was a part of it. I got to sit in on 'Big Brother's Little Brother' every day and I got to see Dermott O'Leary and Davina McCall do their thing as presenters and that for me was the one project I worked on where I knew I wanted to be a presenter.

My Influences

My role model has always been my step dad; we share the same birthday and he has always believed in me and has been hugely encouraging throughout my career. He taught me that "Anything's possible if you put your mind to it." I think having that support and positivity every day is really important especially working in a tough industry like media and that has always helped me to keep going. Musically, I loved a lot of RnB growing up and from a presenter point-of-view, June Sarpong was a massive inspiration when she presented T4 and also Davina McCall who is just brilliant to work with. I also think for women working in the media, seeing Davina presenting while she was pregnant on Big Brother was very inspiring as it showed you can be a mother and have a successful career, which is a very empowering message as it challenges perceptions of what is possible.

The MOBO's!

My biggest career success so far, was when I hosted the red-carpet interviews at the Twentieth Anniversary of the MOBO Awards in 2015. I've always had a good relationship with Kanya King (Founder of the MOBO Awards) having supported the MOBO's for years and having always been passionate about music - it's one of the key events of the calendar year.

A year prior to the event, I reached out to Kanya and said "I'm not sure if you've already got your presenters sorted but I would really love to do this." I sent her my show reel and I told her that if she needed a crew I could also come with my own crew. "I am ready to roll!" and so she put me in contact with the people I needed to keep informed.

Every so often throughout the year, I kept focused on the projects I wanted to film and every time I filmed something new, I reconnected with the relevant people and updated them with what I was doing so that I stayed on their radar.

Two months before the MOBO's, I was working at the first-ever pre-MOBO Awards Show and they offered me the opportunity to do it. I couldn't believe it! Little did they know that in my bedroom I had a vision board and a list of goals that I wanted to achieve and presenting on the red carpet at the MOBO's was always an ambition of mine and one of the goals I set for myself. In my head I already knew the dress I was going to wear, the questions I was going to ask. I knew my opening introduction of what I was going to say. I always knew I was going to be there and so that, by far was my most amazing and successful moment.

Pursuing My Dream
I had decided to leave my job at Disney, where I was

a Publicity Manager for three years. On the outside, people would have thought I was very successful in what I did but on the inside, it felt as though I wasn't really doing what I knew I was always capable of doing and I didn't feel as though I should be there. So I took a massive leap of faith and left. People were really shocked because I left a well-paid and secure job with loads of benefits with nothing lined up but I did this because I believed in myself and because I really wanted to be a presenter.

I spent a month writing a strategy looking at all the things that I'm passionate about, events that excited me which I wanted to cover and I went through my list of contacts that I'd built up over the years and used my network to build a plan of how I would make it happen for myself.

I had a lot of pressure from a responsibility point-of-view, as I have a young son and still had to pay his nursery fees and find some income while still trying to pursue my dream. I got through this by the support of my family, really listening to myself, reading inspirational books and focusing on reaching my targets.

Happiness Jar
Every day I have breakfast with my son no matter what. It's a really special moment between us, as after we've eaten we'll write on post-it notes, the date and what we're thankful for each day. We don't show each other; we then fold it up and put it in the 'Happiness Jar.' The idea is that in a years' time when it's full, we can get

them out and see all the things that made us happy. It's important to me that I teach my son gratitude and mindfulness and I believe this helps him to be thankful and to appreciate the small things in life.

Finding My Balance

My work schedule can differ depending on what project I'm working on so if I'm broadcasting (and not doing any red-carpet events) I'll take my son to school, go to the gym for a yoga and cardio class, have lunch and then go to the studio and broadcast live on the radio on various drive-time shows including BBC Cambridge and Smooth FM between 3-7pm. I keep the weekends free to do things together as a family and catch-up with friends.

Income differs depending on what the projects are; Usually you have a day-rate or half a day's rate or your agent negotiates the rate for you dependant on what the role is - whether it's a red-carpet event, a segment on TV, radio broadcasting or a voice-over for an advert. It's not loads of money but if you get a certain amount of big jobs in a year, then it can be quite lucrative. If you're a presenter on a prime-time show, say like Dermot on the 'X Factor' and the whole of the country is watching it, then yes you are going to be raking it in!

Pitfalls to Avoid

My number one thing for people wanting to work in the media, would be to refuse to work for free. A lot of the time, jobs are offered for free and there is this expectation that if you really want it, you'll do it for free which I would personally discourage because it's really difficult for people to support themselves financially if they are working for free. This industry makes enough money to pay everyone, no matter what level they are at in their career.

Working in media is a very 'word-of-mouth' and 'who you know' industry so be really mindful that whatever job you go into whether you're a production runner, assistant or researcher always look for things that need doing to make a good impression. Don't wait for someone to ask you to do it. People will acknowledge that you're the person who gets things done it and that you're an asset to the team, which will put you in good stead for your next job.

Secret to Securing Your Next Job
To work in media, I would say you have to be a people's person and a networker. It's about people working together to tell stories. It's really important that you're relaxed with people as drinks after work often become conversations about your next project. I don't view anybody that does what I do as competition. Everyone defines success differently but I like to think that there's enough space for everybody to be successful.

Education
I think having my degree definitely helped me to get interviews as it was really admired at the time when I graduated but now having gone full circle, if I was thinking about going to university again I wouldn't because in television production it is more about work experience rather than academic qualifications, so I

would save myself getting into all of that debt. Instead, I would look up the production companies of shows that I watch that most excite me and contact them to see if they were looking for runners and I would get in that way to build up my experience.

Also, go into the building! You'll be surprised how so few people physically walk into a company's premises and say "I would really love to work here, here is my CV who should I give it to?" A lot of the time people really respect that tenacity.

TOP TIPS

Do your research and check the websites of the production companies that make the shows you really enjoy. Also, look out for events organised by Industry leaders such as The Royal Television Society, Bafta and the BFI. They run networking events which are usually free and you can listen/speak to people in the industry about how they got in. Follow the key people you admire on Twitter and join LinkedIn to find out about further opportunities. And finally, practice your craft! If you're hanging around waiting for these opportunities to come to you then you're not going to be ready, whereas if you're practicing the whole time then when the opportunities do come your way, you're good to go.

Take A Small Step Forward Today
Ask yourself why you want to work in this industry and what are you proactively doing yourself to make it happen? They'll be a million reasons why you're not

where you want to be yet but you have to take control of your own life to make it happen. What small step can you do today to get you one step closer to where you want to be?

I WOULD LIKE TO BE REMEMBERED AS...

Someone who inspired others to believe in themselves.

RIA HEBDEN PATHWAY PIT STOP

• Listen to yourself, read inspirational books and focus on reaching your targets
• The Happiness Jar
• Refuse to work for free
• Always look for things that need doing
• It's about working with people to tell stories
• Continue to practice your craft so that you are ready for when opportunities come your way
• What small step can you take today to get you one step closer to where you want to be

RIA HEBDEN CONTACT DETAILS

Twitter: @Riahebden
Instagram: @Riahebden
Website: www.riahebden.com
YouTube: Ria YouTube Channel

DARI SAMUELS

Radio Producer

'What I am more focused on than the success is the process.'

Dari Samuels Prelude

Dari Samuels is a creative, versatile and experienced multimedia producer, making radio programmes at the BBC for fans of urban music. He has delivered record audience figures for two of the BBC Radio 1xtra's leading shows. (1xtra Breakfast & MistaJam) and produced the stations first online video to generate a million views. He is now the Editor of the BBC Radio 1Xtra.

DARI SAMUELS INTERVIEW

I'm Dari Samuels, a lifelong music fan and a producer for BBC Radio. I've been working at BBC Radio 1Xtra since it launched in 2002.

My Love of Music

I grew up in a household where there was always music playing on a radio or a stereo system. I had older sisters who regularly bought records, so I became a fan of music from an early age and started buying seven-inch singles when I was in primary school. By the time I was in secondary school, I was spending my Saturday afternoons in second hand record shops and exploring different kinds of music, especially hip hop, which really grabbed my attention in the early 1990s.

From there I became 'the music guy' at school, making compilation mixtapes for friends, and then at university. That progressed into me being the DJ at student union events. By the time I graduated I was also dabbling with music journalism and I used to write articles for music websites and magazines.

When I graduated I was in debt but luckily, straight out of university I was offered a job on a recruitment company's graduate training scheme. In theory, this was supposed to be the start of my career where I rode off into the sunset and became 'Mr Corporate', but my heart was never really into that idea. Then, in 2002, the BBC was launching 1Xtra as a new radio station and they were looking to recruit production staff.

I hadn't had that much experience in radio but they were looking for people who also had good music knowledge and so I saw it as an opportunity. I applied for the job and after two interviews I got it; but making that change of career meant that I had to take a big pay cut. I was twenty-four years old at the time and going in at entry level with no experience in professional broadcasting. I got fully trained and had a unique experience of being involved in the launch of a brand-new radio station. There was a lot of energy and excitement around that whole process and that's what propelled me through my early months on the job.

The thing that continues to drive me forward in my work is my passion for music; to represent it in the best possible way, and to provide a great platform for fans of it.

Sense of Identity
I remember in primary school that my family provided the only black pupils there, and in secondary school, there weren't too many black children there either. So, having both parents in my household and having elder sisters very much shaped my identity as a black man and also gave me a kind of structure to my life that I only now acknowledge and understand. I often take for granted the circumstances that I grew up in, but I know now that they gave me a very strong cultural foundation and sense of identity.

There were certain values that were instilled in my

family. For instance, my dad was a teacher, so there was a great deal of importance placed on education; and having since met people who had different family experience to me, I now understand how your family circumstances can play a really strong role in determining the choices you make or the choices your parents make for you.

Consistency is the Key

I think my success lies in my ability to consistently deliver good work and to always be aiming for best practice. I've worked on a number of shows on BBC Radio 1Xtra, whether it's Charlie Sloth, the Breakfast Show or MistaJam. When I produced MistaJam's show, I delivered record listening figures and when I moved to work on the Breakfast Show, I again delivered record figures. I also produced 1Xtra's first online video to generate a million views. But what I am more focused on than these successes is the approach I took to get those results. My thinking is "I know where I'm trying to get to. What's the process that will ensure I have the best chance of getting there?" And once I create or develop that process, that's what I focus on.

If you do the right things I believe you'll get the rewards. You may not always get the recognition or the accolades you deserve, but because your process is effective, you'll always have a consistent high level of performance.

Nowadays a lot of people are focused purely on that end result. They think that posting something on Instagram and getting a million 'likes' is success. I would rather look at it as "What's the best way to be active on

Instagram and ensure that over a period of a month I'm consistently getting a high number of likes."

Staying Ahead of the Game

For my role of producer, I needed to keep abreast of what's going on in the music scene. But a lot of my work is done when I don't think I'm actually working. When I'm out of the office in the real world and seeing what things interest people - I use that on-air for my radio show to make content that I think people will be interested in.

If I'm on the bus and I'm listening to what people are talking about, I'm discovering what really matters in these people's lives. When I hear what they're playing on their phones I get a sense of what tunes are actually resonating with people and what they care about. Being a producer is all about getting the right content at the right time for the right people and giving it to them the way that they want it.

The main part of my job is leading a team to make live radio shows, to structure the shows with guests and regular segments, and to create content that lives outside the shows i.e. social media content, photos, YouTube videos etc. It's very multimedia and I'm responsible for quite a lot.

It involves being inspired by the world, getting thrown stuff by the industry and deciding what's the best cocktail of content to put out there for the audience and make them want to listen and get involved in the show.

Social Media/Online Influence

It's a great source of news, information, and access to artists. It can cut out the bureaucracy of going through an official middle man, and it allows people to get in contact with me directly. What I use it most for is to get a gauge of what people are talking about and what their opinions are. There's so much creativity all the platforms provide that it's easy to be inspired by the energy and the ideas that are out there.

People get music and media from so many different sources, there's no one route to success. The audience has got far more sophisticated in the way they consume music and where they get it from. You can't force things on people because they can always opt out of you. They'll go over to Spotify or read a blog, search on YouTube or view a link someone sent them on Facebook. There's a complicated network of interactions and transfers of music happening, and most of its happening without any money being exchanged.

Now we're in an age where 10 year olds may struggle to understand the concept of paying for music - if they can go on YouTube and type in a song and it comes up and they can listen to it, why would they choose to pay for something they can get for free elsewhere? So the music industry is now having to make music-streaming a profitable business, rather than just the selling of tracks being the only way to make money.

Define Your Goals

Try to get some sort of clarity about what you want to

do. What are your real goals? What are you in it for and what do you want to achieve? Are you looking purely for financial gain or must you enjoy what you're doing? Is it about making a difference to other people through your work or is it is about you getting a certain level of status for yourself?

You have to be as clear as possible about your motives and what you're trying to get out of it, and use that to focus your energy. Otherwise you'll have dreams and it's just a dream until you break it down into goals. Ultimately if you're looking to get paid in any field of work, I think it's important to realise you need to be professional and you need to have a level of expertise. Competence is essential if you are trying to progress at anything.

Adaptability
The consumer landscape and culture in general is always evolving, so you have to be adaptable to people's changing tastes, attitudes and values. You have to be flexible, understand and appreciate other people's perspectives, and find ways of tapping into that. So be open-minded in your approach.

For example, for Charlie Sloth's daytime radio show, we made a spoof freestyle rap video for R.S (Roll Safe – comedic character played by Kayode Ewumi). A colleague had sent me a link to R.S' Hood Documentary' online video. I'd watched it and at first didn't really appreciate it's humour, but I could see that its popularity was growing fast. I could appreciate that

I'm older than my radio show's target audience and so there are things that they'll love and I won't because that stuff isn't being made with me in mind. But I saw from the comments and the huge number of views that people were connecting with it. So I went to my assistant producer and said "let's do something with him. Do your thing and make it happen." The "R.S. Fire in the Booth" video became 1Xtra's second most popular YouTube video ever, with 5million+ views in a few months.

Grasping Opportunities

In the sector, there's a wide range of salaries, but they start from low. I was lucky in terms of the timing of when I entered the industry. For the average person, it will mean interning, volunteering to get some experience and hoping for an entry level production assistant role.

For instance, if you're a runner working in television production, you're in the same room as the director, producer and actor. You have the chance to network and make of that opportunity the most you can. Once you're in the room, how can you impress the right people and get the next gig or the next step up? You might be the most talented person but it doesn't mean you'll get the job. Talent isn't always enough. You have to learn to develop the ability to sell yourself and demonstrate your talents to those in a position to influence your career.

Education is Invaluable

I've got a degree in Management Studies and so I have a

theoretical understanding of how successful businesses are run and I have an insight into how things at work could be improved. With getting a degree, I think it's less about what you study and more about the fact that you dedicated 3 years to something and saw it through to the end.

Going to university teaches you self-discipline as you have to manage your own study time and social life. Overall, higher education is invaluable and arms you with knowledge, tools and life skills. Without a certain level of education, I think you are putting yourself at a serious disadvantage in the work market. Trying to 'blag' your way through without having the knowledge can only get you to a certain level, and will ultimately get you found out.

TOP TIPS

For any job you want, if you're smart you look at it from the employee's point of view. Employers are ideally looking for experience. Demonstrate to them you have the skills, ability and knowledge to be able to do the job. It doesn't mean it has to be paid experience. Nowadays, media content is easy to create and you can do it from your bedroom - all you need is a smart phone and you can start creating content. Then it's all about how focused you are and how seriously you take it.

If someone's going to pay you to do a job, you've got to be worth being paid. It's not a charity situation. Some people get hook-ups because they know the right people - it happens, but I'd recommend focusing on building a track record of delivering quality work and gaining the trust and respect of the people you work with. If you're good at what you do, you may not make a killing but you'll be able to make a good living in whatever your profession is.

I WOULD LIKE TO BE REMEMBERED...

Positively, regardless of what I'm remembered for doing, I want the impact to be positive and lasting.

DARI SAMUELS PATHWAY PIT STOP

• Deliver good work and aim for best practice
• Be focused on doing something well rather than the success
• Try to get some clarity as to what it is you want to do
• Keep abreast with what's going on musically and what topics are resonating with the people
• Be adaptable and open minded in your approach to people's tastes attitudes and values.
• Demonstrate your talents to those in position of influence
• Education is essential otherwise you're putting yourself at a serious disadvantage.
• Get yourself experience – all you need is a phone and you can start creating content
• If someone's going to pay you, you've got to be worth being paid.

DARI SAMUELS CONTACT DETAILS

TWITTER: @DariSamuels
INSTAGRAM: @DariSamuels

MICHAEL SANI

Social Entrepreneur

'If money is your only goal you're never going to be fulfilled.'

Michael Sani Prelude

Michael Sani is a social entrepreneur who co-founded Bite the Ballot in 2010 with the help of staff and students at Wilmington Enterprise college and is a member of the Ashoka Fellowship organisation. He was famously quoted by the then U.S President Barack Obama as an 'agent for change'.

MICHAEL SANI INTERVIEW

My name is Michael Sani, I am a Social Entrepreneur and currently leading the Bite The Ballot movement.

Creating Bite the Ballot

When I first started Bite the Ballot I was a school teacher back at the time of the 2010 general election – the idea was born out of frustration at having no intention of voting at the age of twenty-seven, and quickly realising that every student that could vote, wasn't going to participate either. It was only then that I had the realisation that we're failing people if we're not truly informing them of how to be active citizens and the role that they can play in their future.

So, I co-created a project with other members of staff and students that in the first year and a half was a just a lunch time club which was very much solution focused, looking at some of the issues in society that young people were facing and didn't feel were fair and thinking about how we would change them. We mainly looked at engagement and education and this feeling of hope that would ripple if enough of us believe that we can create change. The hurdles started there and then from the lack of support from the head teacher and the senior leadership team and no resources for me to scale up the project that really made me hit a crossroad. So, I left my job. I forced myself into this space because I found a purpose and believed in the outcome. I've always been someone who's wanted to do something special with my life and wanted it to count for something.

My Role Models

During my childhood, I had actor role models who I looked up to because of the portfolio of characters they could play such as Jack Nicholson and Robert De Niro. They were actors that I aspired to emulate because they were really diverse and could portray a whole variety of emotions.

I also had the business side – I idolised Richard Branson, especially when you learn the early stages of the hurdles he's had to overcome, where he's got to and what he's done. They were my people in the limelight that I looked up to.

I looked up to my grandad but for different reasons. As a husband, he wasn't a great man, he provided for his family but had many regrets related to his marriage and relationship with my nan. But as a principled man that lived through wars, and shared so many of his regrets with me, I guess he became a role model of mine because it made me think I want to live as best I can and not have regrets.

Travelling Around the World

Hands down my biggest success was travelling around the world when I was twenty-three years old. I was the first person in our group of pals on the estate in South East London to go to university. I quickly became aware of difference and how rich it is to share halls of residence with a skateboarder from Brighton to a guy from Venezuela and everything else in-between, I really embraced the beauty of diversity and different people and interests.

After I finished university I went to work for the Bank of America. I had this vision of "I'll become a Trader" and I was progressing well at the bank and was liked by key people, but after a year and a half I quit because I found the job soul destroying, and that's when I went travelling around the world.

That for me is my greatest accomplishment because it's made me the man I am today. It's made me care about culture and people and difference and understand the importance of values and inter-generational family connections. It also gave me this notion of questioning what is it that makes us happy? You can't go to some countries in the world and be on the road for so long without really fine tuning you as a person. You have these big moments and questions to help you realise what you exist for and what you want from life? I've had success professionally with Bite the Ballot, which went from an idea in a classroom and 6 years later got me name checked by the then United States of America President, Barack Obama. Those moments are clearly defining millstones in my life but outside of a professional environment I always feel our achievements should be about our development as people.

Barack Obama
To see Obama, live in front of you, and just feel his power and energy. Then the next minute he says my name, refers to me as an 'agent for change' and quotes me, I felt the energy and power transfer to me. That day I grew as an individual, as a professional and most importantly the purpose I dedicate my life too. I joked

with friends that 'I had peaked' that was it now... How could I ever experience a sense of achievement as I did that day? It made all the struggles, frustrations and dark days' worth it.

<u>Stand up to Adversity!</u>

In 2012 Bite the Ballot worked with the Cabinet Office. We got offered a project to make some games and resources that would essentially inspire young people to register to vote. We were given some money to do that and targets to reach. I worked with a small team of young citizens to help create these games and then went on the road and tested them. It was hugely successful; in twenty locations, we had put two thousand four hundred people on the electoral roll that had never heard of it. The games were experiential learning and rewarding for the people that had carried it out, and for the people who created them.

When I got back I was introduced to the very cut throat world of Public Departments of Government – we were told "Thank you very much but we'll take it from here, you're not needed anymore." We had given everything and felt that we were the perfect people to carry it on because it wasn't just the games it was the ethos that we were spreading. We could have rolled over and took it but we felt that no government department could replicate this and be able to relate to the people they're trying to reach out too.

So we complained to Nick Clegg, (the then Deputy Prime Minister.) His team challenged the Cabinet Office and in the end, Bite the Ballot got to keep the games and resources but so did the Government. The lesson I learned is that you can't be afraid to stand up to adversity or take on big powerful institutions who are used to brushing people aside, we must spotlight bad practice.

Work Ethic & Routines
It sounds cliché to say but no day is ever the same. Over the last 6 years' things have changed so much, you grow and develop as a team, you scale up, you scale down, you stop, you reflect, you go again!

At Bite the Ballot we have 5-year strategy cycles which start and end from General Election to General Election. My current schedule is Monday, I use as my admin day and time with the team. Tuesday and Friday are my meeting days with external clients, customers, potential partners, stakeholders and interviews. Once a month I'll have a full team catch up where we look at design and finances and then quarterly we'll book in team away days to explore our well-being and how we're personally feeling. It might not always go to plan but partly it's about being strict with yourself.

I make sure I have one day a week off where I'll play golf or go for a walk, as it helps me gather perspective. I can't always be in the trenches and it's important to remove myself from the day to day stuff otherwise people will always look to ask me for my opinion and I want people to do it for themselves.

Ashoka Fellow

I've been very fortunate to become an Ashoka Fellow, an organisation that recognises and supports Social Entrepreneurs. They're three thousand of us around the world and thirty-six in the UK including myself. Working with this network has made me understand how important wellbeing is.

It's important your friends and family get time with you outside of work where you can go and spend quality time and actually be present in their company. It's important you fulfil desires of love and affection. If you're always busy it's not going to happen. Life is about moments and you just need to try and have a balance of having as many as those moments that feed your soul and that are going to be memorable to everyone involved, as well as the long nights and dedicated weeks of work that progress you forward.

Pitfalls to Learn From

Be prepared for the bureaucracy and be resilient, especially if you're going into an area of pursuing social change or social impact.

Appreciate the ability to celebrate failure; it's an amazing concept of learning how not to do something. I felt the first 5 years of Bite the Ballot was an intense game of chess. My naivety in the beginning was recognising that something could change and thinking it's going to happen so easily. That was almost like me throwing my queen straight off the chess board. With the failed moves of the past you know better ways of doing it for the future. Next time around you are prepared for the hurdle and will approach situations differently leaving no stone unturned because you'll have thought through every move. It's all about finding the progress in disappointment.

Finally, delayed gratification; feel good about not seeing your outcome. You might not ever see your goal but feel satisfied that if in two hundred years' time your vision is now reality, history will document you being part of it. Many activists that have created change didn't really understand the concept of their impact in their lifetime. It's appreciation for "I haven't got to see it but one day, one generation will"

Attributes Needed to be Successful

I think for me personally one of the biggest attributes to be successful is to quickly realise it doesn't matter who gets recognition for the outcome as long as the outcome is achieved. Learn when to forgive, sometimes you need to park certain feelings and try and think about the greater good. Another is, truly find a good way of working in collaboration - find people where you all look at it as a collective pot. Everybody puts something in and everybody takes something out and when you find those partners they're the ones to cherish and hold onto.

Money isn't the Prime Goal the Outcome is

For the first few years of my work, I'd invest all I had into the project and I'll take very little out. Now I'm sitting on a salary that is definitely reasonable and above average of 50k but I certainly value myself more than that and when the times right I'll grow my own earnings. For me money is a tool and in the future, I want an abundance to be able to provide for my family and have a level of disposable income where I'll become a philanthropist in my own right. It's only when you progress with a vision or desire with a specific outcome that you suddenly unfold opportunities. When money isn't the prime goal and the outcome is, you'll be surprised how unexpectedly money can follow. My advice is if you add a layer of social impact to the work you're doing the rewards will be endless. If money is your only goal you're never going to be fulfilled.

Education Through Life

My formal education was good I studied Business Management at Southampton Institute. I became quite inspired by what business can be (not what it is) — leadership, strategy, communication and motivation and the theories behind them really interested me. It's a shame the real world of business has the cut throat layer of greed, power and in many cases corruption.

However, it wasn't my formal education that played the biggest part of where I am today. I would say it's my life education, growing up in a South East London estate with very little. You develop a grit and resilience because you haven't got what other people have got and you can't easily get it. You find creative ways of remaining ambitious and allow your hurdles to be the making of you - they are all tests that if passed mean you are always progressing.

TOP TIPS

1. If you're going to go into the area of Social Entrepreneurship, then 9 times out of 10 it will be something that really frustrates you or something you feel a lot of empathy towards - feel the social justice right at your core and dedicate yourself to being part of the solution. Turn those frustrations into opportunities.

2. I would also say never think anything's a waste of time. If it's of interest to you at that point in time and you've got conviction, follow it through. Even if you ridiculed by your friends and family because there is no career in it or it's something that no one else does, do it and do it with conviction. Who knows when you'll draw back on the experience of the people you've met or the avenues you've walked down. "Diversity is a wonderful thing in a variety of ways, celebrate what makes you different"

3. Lastly trust your gut, your intuition will speak to you so listen to it.

Next Steps
I'm going to progress in the idea of digital democracy. I also want to get into the Early Years education space developing, through play, the skills and values of a young citizen. I've recently been made a LEGO Fellow for Re-imagination Learning. I'm one of thirty in the whole world that has been made a fellow, which is quite an honour.

In the future, I want to be an advocate for the

profession of Social Entrepreneurship not only in the promotion of more people considering it but equally in the lobbying, and formal intuitions to recognise it as a career and offer incentives for people to make a positive social impact through their work.

I WOULD LIKE TO BE REMEMBERED...

Alongside other activists that stood up and fought against injustice, believing in equality and the well-being of others. From Martin's Luther King to the Suffragettes. I would like to be regarded as someone who has taken the baton and was dedicated to making progress as best as possible during my time. What stands before me and what those activists didn't have is technology and global connectivity - this is a huge opportunity. I would like to be remembered as somebody who supported the pursuit of happiness and never accepted the unacceptable.

MICHAEL SANI PATHWAY PIT STOP

• Our achievements should be about our development as people
• Don't be afraid to stand up to adversity
• It's important your friends and family get to spend time with you outside of work
• Recognise the importance of your own well-being and mental health
• Appreciate the ability to celebrate failure
• Delayed gratification; Feel good about not seeing your outcome
• Find good ways of working in collaboration

• If money is your only goal you're never going to be fulfilled
• Never think anything's a waste of time

MICHAEL SANI CONTACT DETAILS

Twitter: @BiteTheBallot
Instagram: @MichaelSani
Website: www.bitetheballot.co.uk

CAIRBRE Ó CAIREALLÁIN

Strength & Conditioning Coach

'I judge my success not on trophies or how much I earn, but on the sense of fulfilment that comes with having a positive impact on someone and helping to empower others.'

Cairbre Ó Cairealláin Prelude

Cairbre Ò Caireallain is a Strength and Conditioning Coach at Arsenal Women FC. He joined the club in August 2015 from a background in GAA to work in the Youth Academy at Hale End, before joining the ladies team in January 2016. After graduating from the university of Limerick with an Msc Sports performance in 2013, he undertook the strength and conditioning role with the Limerick Hurling Academy with a focus on the physical development of young players from under-fourteen to under-eighteen level.

CAIRBRE Ó CAIREALLÁIN INTERVIEW

My name is Cairbre Ó Cairealláin, I am originally from Belfast, Ireland and I am the Strength and Conditioning Coach for the Arsenal Woman' Football Team.

How I Started Out

I have always been passionate about sports. I grew up playing Hurling, the national game of Ireland, and was obsessed with getting the best out of myself, and seeing how far I could go with it.

I believe in the importance of re-framing negative experiences; when one door closes, another one opens. During my early twenties I picked up one injury after another, making it difficult to pursue my sporting ambitions. My experience in sport coupled with having these injuries sparked a great interest in me to learn more about the human body, why it breaks down, and how we can resolve pain and build resilience for sports performance. I gradually spent more time personal training/coaching others. I started off coaching GAA teams in Limerick, Ireland, and then moved to the Arsenal Football Club working with the Youth Academy and now currently with the Women' team.

Hurling Hero

I spent my childhood dreaming of emulating my Hurling heroes and one day playing in Croke Park. A huge role model for my brothers and I was Seán Óg Ó hAilpín. He and his family were born in Fiji but grew up in Australia. The family moved to his father's native country, Ireland, when he was 7 years old. He took up Hurling, a sport which he had never seen before. Seán Óg, along with his brothers and sisters, embraced the culture, Gaelic games and the Irish language. Seán Óg played at the highest level for his county and went onto become one the best players of his generation.

I grew up with his poster on my bedroom wall, but was lucky enough to get to know him and play alongside him for a couple of years when I played with Na Piarsaigh in Cork. For me he epitomises what a role model is. On the pitch, there is no ego, just hard work and self-belief. Off the pitch, he is a very selfless character and would do anything for you, that's what makes him such a great ambassador for the values of Gaelic games.

Growing up, I was heavily influenced by my parents, who raised three boys during the turbulence of the troubles in Belfast in the eighties and nineties. They were very passionate about Irish culture and the Irish language, and despite a lot of hostility from those in power at the time, they made it possible for us to grow up and live in a community where our native language was respected and valued. They were amongst a group of volunteers dedicated to the language who formed an Irish language primary school, a secondary school, a newspaper, radio station, theatre company, and cultural centre.

If they sat around the table thinking about these projects, they would have come to realise that they were impossible. Instead, they made it happen, and now there is a thriving and growing Irish language community in Belfast. They lived by strong values and unstoppable drive that inspires me as I continue my professional journey as a coach.

Helping Empower Others

Personally, I judge my success not on trophies or how much I earn, but on the sense of fulfilment that comes with having a positive impact on someone and helping to empower others.

The feeling after a good training session with a current of positive energy in the room there is the sense of satisfaction that comes with working hard towards a collective goal - I get a kick out of that. Being a Strength and Conditioning coach gives me the opportunity to help people to move better, to feel good about themselves and to reach their potential as athletes.

Whether it is working with an elite-level football team like the Arsenal Ladies, a twelve-year-old who plays for the local Hurling team, or an office worker who just wants to get in shape, the goal is ultimately the same: helping people lead better lives through training and movement. Bringing awareness to; and developing the physical nature of the human body in an engaging and enjoyable manner, with the positive mental and emotional benefits that come with that, is incredibly gratifying. I take great pleasure from contributing in whatever way I can to the quality of lives of my players; I am extremely lucky to be in a position to do so and hope to continue improving my coaching skills.

Overcoming My Injuries

When I was twenty one I broke my foot, the following year I injured my knee, and a couple of years later required hip arthroscopic surgery. So, the constant battle of rehab and working towards good physical health, along with the mental strain of an injury, was extremely challenging for me.

At the time Hurling at the best level possible was my primary goal and focus, and suddenly that was taken away from me. Eventually, I learned to deal with this adversity and to accept things as they were. The experience helped me develop a broader perspective on life and strengthened my mental resilience.

Work Ethic & Routines

I co-ordinate the Athletic Development program for the Arsenal Women FC first team, with the goal of instilling a culture of physical preparation within the squad, enhancing athletic performance on the field while helping to keep players healthy and injury-free.

At times the role can become a juggling act, with so many important variables to consider and manage. Players need to improve their movement competency, strength, power, speed, fitness, but they also need to be fresh and ready to compete every Sunday. To ensure this, a lot of time and effort is put into the training planning process as well as in monitoring the player's response to training. This includes regularly taking measurements from players that assess fatigue, using GPS technology to measure physical outputs such as distance covered and speed of running during training.

I take the team through a warm-up before every training session, I run the team gym sessions, as well as the on-field speed and conditioning work on-field. As everyone is different, an important part of this process is getting to know each player, how much training they can tolerate, and what exercises they respond well to in the gym. Building strong professional relationships with your athletes is necessary so that they trust the process and follow the plan.

Rehabbing injuries is a big part of the job which requires careful individual attention. Being injured and not able to compete is very frustrating for players, and so aside from prescribing specific exercises and training programs to help the physical recovery, supporting the player's mental wellbeing is equally important.

As players feed of your energy and enthusiasm as a coach, self-care plays an important role in my ability to give my best to the team every day. I follow a morning routine which includes meditation, a movement and mobility routine, and 5 minutes of journaling which helps to set my intentions for the day ahead and kick things off on a positive note.

What it Takes to be The Best

The journey to success and to becoming the best at something doesn't necessarily lend itself to a balanced lifestyle. Whether it is the pursuit of excellence in sport, music, or career; the commitment and investment it takes to become the best requires an extraordinary investment of time and effort, and that's probably the case with my role at the minute. At the same time, I don't think we should take things too seriously or worry about things too much. The world is full of people living in a state of chronic stress, so it is important for me to switch off and enjoy life when possible.

Control Your Ego

In the Strength and Conditioning world, especially in the age of the internet, there are a lot of keyboard warriors. It's easy to sit behind your computer, anonymously criticising and bashing other coaches, it makes us feel superior and better about ourselves. The essence of being a good Strength and Conditioning coach, however, is real life coaching and helping people improve. It has to be about the athlete and not yourself, which means controlling your ego. A "know it all" attitude is self-limiting so be open to learning and enhancing your knowledge and skillset. Humility goes a long way, so my advice to young coaches would be to remember that there is no one way of doing things and that you don't have all the answers.

Separating Myself from The Competition

The passion I have for optimizing health and performance, as well as a genuine interest in the people I work with has stood me well as a coach. I have a strong willingness to learn and improve my understanding of the complexities of the human body.

The field of athletic development is constantly evolving, which makes it necessary to always stay in touch with the research and evidence of best practice. Good coaches are really perpetual students themselves, learning from their own experiences and other great coaches, synthesising new information, and applying it in their own way. As a coach, it does not serve you well being a textbook expert without the practical application of that knowledge. Real life coaching and movement practice is where the magic happens.

At the same time, you must live it on a practical level yourself. Knowing what it feels like to complete a gruelling conditioning program, having your own regular movement practice and strength training routine. Having this personal experience strengthens your message as the strength and conditioning coach. Put an emphasis on creating positive energy and enthusiasm that enables those who work with you to feed off your passion.

Focus on Coaching and Not The Money
Strength and Conditioning is such a broad field that you could be coaching 8-year-olds, a Premier League star, or retired pensioners who want to keep fit. If you are passionate about this career I think it's about coaching wherever you can to begin with, being patient and focus on the process of coaching the person in front of you rather than the outcome of getting that big job. Coaches are in a privileged position and we must appreciate this no matter who the individual or team is under our guidance.

The likelihood of eventually earning a higher income may be higher if you are intrinsically motivated by and passionate about the coaching process, rather than being primarily motivated by financial gain.

Find a Mentor
I certainly benefited from doing my A-Levels and studying Sport and Exercise Sciences in university. I think that any goal that requires perseverance and hard work can be a worthwhile process. University develops many useful skills, it improves your capacity to take on and critique new information, it forces you to be

organised with projects and deadlines. However, I don't believe that there is one set path to being successful in life, having a good career or making a positive impact on society. Particularly now in the age of the internet there is more accessibility to knowledge than ever, giving us the opportunity to learn and apply this knowledge with first-hand experience. I can foresee a time when internships, interpersonal skills, work ethic, willingness to learn and improve will be valued as much as a university degree.

Finding a mentor you can learn from is invaluable. I did this through surrounding myself with like-minded people, and learning from great strength and conditioning coaches, without even meeting them. Nowadays we have the luxury of the internet available to us; we can seek out the best coaches online and listen to their podcasts, interviews and videos. Reading books will always be one of the best ways to expand your knowledge.

The more you understand the principles of how the human body works and self-organises, the more you can use your own creativity to develop novel ways of challenging the body and exploring the infinite variations of movement that we are capable off.

TOP TIPS

It is a cliché but no less true that you really need to have a passion for whatever you spend your time on, as this will drive your ambition to grow and persevere on the hard days. When it comes to Strength and Conditioning, always be confident in what you're coaching – if you don't have confidence in yourself, nobody else will. When you win the trust of your athletes, they will buy into your methods of training and of building the positive habits needed to become a great athlete.

I WOULD LIKE TO BE REMEMBERED AS...

"People don't care how much you know until they know how much you care". I always like to remind myself of this quote, which has great wisdom, particularly as a coach. I hope I'll be remembered as someone who did care, and as someone who worked hard at doing the best job possible and adding value to the players under my care.

CAIRIBE O'CARREALLAIN PATHWAY PIT STOP

• The journey to success and to becoming the best at something doesn't necessarily lend itself to a balanced lifestyle.
• The essence of being a good Strength and Conditioning coach is helping people improve.
• It does not serve you well being a textbook expert. On some level, you must live it on a practical level yourself.
• Control your ego. A "know it all" attitude can be self-limiting.
• Find a mentor and surround yourself with like-minded people
• Research and learn new ways to do things - Listen to podcasts, interviews and videos of the best coaches out there to build up your knowledge.

• If you don't have confidence in yourself, nobody else will.

CAIRIBE O'CARREALLAIN CONTACT DETAILS

Website: www.feedmestrength.com

DINA ASHER-SMITH

Track & Field Athlete

'You have to work hard to get the results you want.'

Dina Asher-Smith Prelude

Dina Asher-Smith is a British Sprinter who holds the British records for both the 100 metres and 200 metres. Inter 4 x 100 metres relay, she won Bronze medals at the 2016 Olympic Games and the 2013 World Championships. She is also the 2016 European Champion at the 200 metres, the 2015 World Junior Champion at the 100 metres and the 2013 European Junior Champion at the 200 metres.

DINA ASHER-SMITH INTERVIEW

My name is Dina Asher-Smith and I am an athlete. I specialise in the 100m and 200m where I am the current British record holder with personal best times of 10.99 seconds and 22.07 seconds.

My Journey into Athletics
My parents very much influenced my love of sport. From an early age, I've always been active, whether that was going for long bike rides or playing golf in the garden with my dad, or playing hockey and watching it on TV with my mum. From then, I had always wanted to be an athlete but I would use that word in the more general sense rather than doing athletics by itself. At a younger age, I used to do athletics but also dancing, swimming, board diving, hockey and netball every week. I got into athletics via Cross Country. My primary school entered me for my borough's Cross Country championships and I won. From there I joined my local athletics club, Blackheath and Bromley and I just kept coming back.

Girls Love Beyoncé
My hero was Beyoncé. It's an odd hero for an athlete to have, mainly because she's an entertainer, but when she is considered for her power, strength and work ethic - she makes a pretty good role model.

Rio Olympics 2016
The proudest moment of my career so far was most probably getting a bronze medal in the 4x100m in Rio. It was something that, as a squad, we had worked so hard

towards and really believed that as long as we trusted each other we would be okay – so to achieve that was amazing. And it feels great to be the British 100m and 200m record holder! It also feels a bit weird, because in a way I can't believe that somehow it happened to be me!

Taking Nothing for Granted

Well the main one that served as a learning point for me was when I missed out on getting into the Secondary Grammar School that I wanted to go to by one mark. In the exam itself, I distinctly remember making silly mistakes, leaving answers blank and not checking my work, which ultimately led to a hugely upsetting disappointment when the results came through. Luckily enough, a few weeks later they extended the entry and I got in but from that I learnt a long-term lesson – to always work hard and take nothing for granted – which has stuck with me ever since.

Insight into Work Ethic & Routines

Pretty boring if I'm being honest haha! I am still at university, so I'll go to Uni (King's college London) in the morning for lectures and to do reading and work on assignments, and then I will run home to have a quick power nap, eat a snack and then head out to training in the evening. I get home at around 9pm, so then I will eat and relax before I go to bed.

Having Understanding Friends

I'm fortunate that I have really understanding friends. Every race they're always watching on TV and have obviously been supporting me long before I became an international. They have seen all the hard work I've put in and believe in my journey – which means that when I plead to move the time we will meet to after training, or I can't meet up with them one day they completely understand. But on my side, I always make an effort to see them. I love my friends and seeing them is a major part of what makes me happy, I just work hard to maintain a balance to achieve the best of both worlds.

PITFALLS TO AVOID

The fact that your fate in the profession, and elite sport in general, is so unpredictable, you have to make sure you have some form of plan B or alternative just in case it doesn't go the way you want. In athletics, you're always just one bad injury or perhaps one funding drop away from potentially having to find another career path so it is wise to not put all your eggs in one basket. You may be top of the world today but tomorrow you may never be able to run again. This is why I was working so hard to get a degree whilst trying to make the Olympic team.

Attributes Needed to be A Successful
Dedication, resilience and unwavering self-belief. You have to work hard to get the results you want but at the same time be mentally tough enough to see the bigger picture and keep pushing when everything isn't going according to plan.

Represent
The rewards in athletics are not really about money. I work to have the honour to compete for my country which when I do I first and foremost represent myself,

my coach and my parents. And then I feel like I represent the little underdog when I compete internationally. The person that may be able to do well, but certainly not a favourite - I try to emphasise that it's what happens on the day that counts and that track - just like life in general - is very unpredictable.

<u>Education</u>
Through my education, I've learnt so much! The true value of hard work, persistence and concentration. To research and understand matters for myself rather than just taking someone's word for it. But I would say that it's more the qualities that I've gained along the way that's had the biggest influence.

TOP TIPS

I will keep it simple and just give one. I will say to just go for it and give it your all! With some things, you only have one chance to truly make it count, so I would say don't hold back and make sure you give it 110%!

FUTURE ASPIRATIONS

After managing to get onto the podium in Rio I would love to become a consistent medalist on the world stage.

I WOULD LIKE TO BE REMEMBERED AS...

An incredibly hard worker.

DINA ASHER-SMITH PATHWAY PIT STOP

• Always work hard and take nothing for granted
• Don't put all your eggs in one basket – have a Plan B
• Be dedicated, resilient and have unwavering self-belief
• Sometimes you only have one chance to truly make it count so don't hold back and give it 110%

DINA ASHER-SMITH CONTACT DETAILS

Twitter: @dinaashersmith
Instagram: @dinaashersmith
Website: www.dinaashersmith.com

ROSA HOSKINS

Writer/Blogger

'Be confident in your opinion that what you have to say is interesting.'

Rosa Hoskins Prelude
Rosa Hoskins is the daughter of the late Bob Hoskins and grew up hanging out on movie sets with her dad. She is a writer and actress and has worked as an editor and stylist as well as writing screenplays and producing for TV and film. She also runs a blog called Haute Hoskins.

Rosa Hoskins Interview

My name is Rosa Hoskins and I am a Writer/Blogger and Personal Stylist.

Going Full Circle

I started off as a jobbing actress and I had mixed success, sometimes it went really well sometimes it didn't. My experience of the acting world is very typical of what most people go through and I found that eventually the insecurity, the not knowing and having a career of always coming second - while loads and loads of girls who I competed with for the same part ended up getting the role and that becoming their big break - was so frustrating. So, I thought there has to be something else I can do that's interesting, artistic, creative and fulfilling where I don't have to give up on acting but that can give me a nicer life. So, I started doing personal styling for a company I was working for and weirdly it was styling that took me into writing. I began to write the company's online content for them and from there I got offered a job at a fashion magazine and then I went out on my own. My writing has now gone full circle and my different strands of work have come together as one cohesive thing.

My Influences

My parents and daughters who are friends of the family that were 10 years older than me such as Polly and Morella. They both value their intelligence and talent first above and beyond all the things women are taught to value themselves on. Who you are and what you're capable of is more important than what you like. My dad was a huge role model to me. He was so unequivocally himself. He never tried to fit into someone else's view of what he should be. My mum in that she's got a real grace about herself, she's very thoughtful and charming and it comes from a place of genuine kindness and generosity. Also, my Grandmother too. Even though she died when I was really young she was super stylish and had an amazing spirit.

My Dad Bob Hoskins

My book 'It's All Going Wonderfully Well' was the hardest and most difficult thing I've ever had to do. I was writing about my dad during the very early stages of grieving and I would find myself weeping at my laptop.

My dad was Bob Hoskins; he was an actor and he was diagnosed with a very aggressive form of Parkinson's in 2011. I originally thought to write a book about him back in 2012 because as I saw him lose his memory, I wanted to do something that could preserve his memories and keep them all together.

It became very clear that the project was too hard to do while he was still around. Focusing on his past glory and how he was when he was well whilst watching him fall apart was too painful. So, I shelved the project until I had my friend/co-author Richard help write it with me as I wouldn't have been able to do it without his support.

The achievement of getting it done came through

persistence and I think that's the key to anything; the ability to keep going. If you start something don't stop until it's completed and don't give up.

Overcoming Dyslexia
Because I was really dyslexic I was at the bottom of my class for nearly everything in school. Some of the teachers were really patronising saying that I don't read enough and that I wouldn't get good enough grades and there were certain things academically that I would not be able to achieve and for a really long time I thought that I was stupid and so being a writer was something that never occurred to me as being an option.

It took me a long time to shake that off and find the confidence to know this is something I could do and do it well and in the end those teachers couldn't have been more wrong because here I am today a writer and published Author. If you've got a burning desire to do something and you know you're good at it then you've got to stick with it.

Building and Maintaining Relationships
If you're a freelancer like me and you work from home, you have to be quite strict with yourself. I've found it important to go out into the real world and meet people because with blogging you can be stuck behind your computer all day. There are lots of networking events and blogger parties/clubs you can join online. www.meetup.com is excellent and Guardian do master classes and have some brilliant lectures and City Lit Adult college do some really good writing courses. If it

doesn't cost you anything go along, take your card and get talking to people!

Anyone that's looking to set up a blog or have internet presence you have to have persistence and keep doing it regularly.

I try to make an effort to balance work and home. It's really important to make time for your friends and family no matter how busy you are. It only takes an hour to go and have a coffee with someone or to have a phone conversation with them. If you maintain those relationships with the people who mean a lot to you, that have supported you and that have history with you, it makes you feel more grounded.

Pitfalls to Avoid

There are some very unscrupulous people on the internet and because internships have become an integral part in starting a career, companies very often end up getting people to work for free. To a certain degree you have to kind of except it and do your best to make it work whatever way you can, but I don't always agree with this. So, my advice would be don't be fooled into doing too much work for free. Do it for a little while but know that there's a cut-off point and so after the first year or two of writing free articles say "No I've got enough experience; I'm going to charge you now." Don't under sell yourself, negotiate but start high. You might feel shy at first but you have to know your worth. Don't fall into the trap of being the eternal intern.

<u>Attributes Needed to Be A Successful Blogger</u>

There are technical things you can do in terms of spreading your sphere of influence. That can be through partnering up with somebody who you have similar synergy with or contributing to someone else's blog.

What makes a blogger successful is not always quantifiable sometimes their just really watchable or likeable. A lot of bloggers in fashion and beauty focus on reviewing products but I realised that I'm more of a writer and what I have to say is a bit broader.

I like to do social commentary and talk about issues on feminism and the current political climate. I would suggest you need to develop your own authentic voice, know what it is that you have to say, don't worry about trying to sound different or be different, just be authentic as authenticity always makes you unique.

Contribute to the world/conversation especially if you've had an experience that people can relate with. Be confident in your opinion that what you have to say is interesting, that people do want to hear your point of view and that they value your suggestions.

Make yourself an expert in something. So, if I was a hair blogger and I've tried twenty different hairsprays and there was one in particular that stood out I would recommend it to viewers. It's likely my audience would be more inclined to buy it. So, don't try to be something to everyone, be everything to someone.

It's a New Phenomenon

It's very difficult to say what people could expect to earn because the internet is constantly evolving and blogging is still quite a new phenomenon. There are some bloggers who are superstar bloggers and earn millions. The reality is most people don't get that but it's not to say you can't earn a good living. It's very competitive for a lot of the big bloggers to land a deal or get an advertising contract with a company. A lot of beauty and fashion bloggers focus on reviewing products; So, a company may send them products and they'll review them and they might earn money by getting a kick back by way of a customer going through their website to buy a product and they'll get a cut out of that. Or they may sign up with a company and all the content they write up for that brand they'll get paid for.

My revenue comes from projects and opportunities I get commissioned to do from people who have looked at the blog and then they say can you write this for us. My blog is shop window where people can come to me, see what I look like, see what I wrote and then book my services through that. I would suggest start with something you have an authentic passion for and then gradually think how can I make money out of this?

TOP TIPS

I don't think that my degree and my level of education necessarily applies to what I'm doing now. I'm sure they'll eventually be courses on how to be a blogger or a Youtuber if there aren't already now.

The beauty of blogging is that you don't have to have any money to do it and if you have access to a computer you can do it in your own time.

Recognise your strengths, don't dismiss your interests and have faith in yourself and time. Have your plan and set your goals but be open to whatever else may come your way by playing the cards you've been dealt.
A small piece of advice I would give to any young person taking exams, if you don't do well in your GCSE's, BTEC's or A Levels don't think that those results are permanent because there not. It can feel like a label but it doesn't define you.

I WOULD LIKE TO BE REMEMBERED AS...

Someone who loved, was honest, was a good friend, sister, wife and eventually mother, and that my work has contributed something to the human experience which helped people feel connected.

ROSA HOSKINS PATHWAY PIT STOP

- Persistence is the key to anything
- If you've got the burning desire to do something and you know you're good at it then stick with it.
- It only takes one hour to have a coffee or phone conversation with friends and family
- Don't fall into the trap of being the eternal intern
- Develop your own authentic voice and make yourself an expert in something
- As long as you have access to a computer you can do blogging and writing in your own time
- Recognise your strengths, don't dismiss your interests and have faith in yourself and time.
- Have a plan, set goals and don't let any negative labels define you.

ROSA HOSKINS CONTACT DETAILS

Twitter: @Hautehoskins
Instagram: @Hautehoskins
Website: www.hautehoskins.com

Acknowledgments

"Readth make the man wise" for as long as I can remember that was the mantra my mother preached to me from a very young age. She was always determined to provide the best upbringing she could for both me and my younger sister whilst being a single parent. I know there were many times she must have felt like literally pulling her hair out as quite often my sister and I weren't best behaved, but words can't describe the amazing job she did of keeping a roof over our heads, food in the fridge, clothes on our back and many family holidays that will live long in our memories.

When I was in primary school struggling both in English and maths my mum somehow found the extra money to hire not one but two private tutors each week to help advance my level of development in those subject areas. Now, twenty years later I have written my first book and I owe this all to you as without your commitment and determination not to fail me and help provide the very best that you could, this project wouldn't be a reality. Thank you for everything Mum I love you always and forever.

I would personally like to thank all of the twenty-one contributors who have participated in my book. I am sincerely humbled and deeply appreciative of you all for giving up your time and sharing your experiences and believing in my project. None of this would have been possible without your support, involvement and contribution. Each one of your stories is unique and special and I thank you from the bottom of my heart for helping my idea become a reality.

For me personally I was very humbled and honoured to see the turnout of young people who attended my focus group on 11th September 2015, especially when they were all giving up free time on a Saturday morning assisting me! You guys contributed so much to the workshop in such a short space of time and gave me a huge amount of insight as to how I could make this book authentic, interactive, purposeful and exciting to read. So, special shout outs to Alycia, Javan, Javente, Miracle, Asad, Martel, Tolu, Kane and Amir. My gratitude and thanks goes out to you all as this wouldn't have been possible without your participation and input.

Special praise goes to you Deborah, for mentoring me throughout the last 7 years on the true core values of Youth Work and how to play an active role in effecting positive change in young people's lives.

Ben, thank you for your support and guidance throughout the past two years in helping me to keep on track and chip away at the project bit by bit up to its completion. Your assistance, encouragement and mentoring has turned my project into a reality and I am forever grateful for all that you have done and taught me throughout this process.

To the wonderful and beautiful Porsche, you have been there since day one of the project. You have supported me by dedicating your time, patience, advice and feedback in helping me to reach this moment. Your unwavering belief in me is appreciated more than you could ever know. There's no one else better I could have shared this journey with.

I must give a massive shout out to all my friends who have not only encouraged and supported me with my book but have been there for me throughout my highs and lows of the last fifthteen years. Big up Kareem, Ryan, Kyle, Michael, Segun, Nathan, Rachel, Alycia, Danny, Voyland and Safa, you all embrace the true definition of friendship.

Last, but not least my siblings! There's nothing else I like doing than just kicking back, bussing joke and chilling with you all. Whether we're all together in one room or we're meeting up individually, you all remind me to keep myself grounded in life, to always appreciate family, celebrate moments and live every day to its fullest and take each lesson as a blessing. To Andrette, Tarnya, Aaron, Byron, Lorrae, Reanna and Taryn, I love you all dearly and you all inspire me to reach greater heights. I dedicate this book in remembrance to our brother Lewis, gone but never forgotten and forever in our hearts.

Notes: Planning Your Future

Notes: Planning Your Future

Notes: Planning Your Future